Classic Steam

1966

CLASSIC STEAM

1966

A month-by-month journey around Britain in pursuit of steam

Roger Siviter ARPS

Silver Link Publishing Ltd

First published in August 1996

British Library Cataloguing in Publication Data

A catalogue record for this book is available from the British Library.

ISBN 1 85794 058 X

Silver Link Publishing Ltd
Unit 5
Home Farm Close
Church Street
Wadenhoe
Peterborough PE8 5TE
Tel (01832) 720440
Fax (01832) 720531
e-mail: pete@slinkp-p.demon.co.uk

Printed and bound in Great Britain

The general month-by-month information was researched by Tricia Adams, except for the shed closure and locomotive withdrawal information, which was supplied by Chris Banks.

Monday 26 September
Frontispiece On the Halesowen-Old Hill branch Class '2MT' 2-6-0 No 46442 descends the bank into Halesowen with a goods from Stourbridge Junction. Twelve days later the 2-6-0 was withdrawn from service at Tyseley shed (see page 147).

Tuesday 13 September
Below Garsdale Viaduct, with '8F' 2-8-0 No 48622 heading north with a mixed goods train. This is so obviously a snatched shot that at the time I thought 'What a so-and-so!' for including the car. I have published this picture before and was able to crop out the car and still have a pleasant picture. But when Silver Link's editor, Will Adams, asked me if I had a picture of the car I used in 1966, I was pleased to be able to come up with this shot of my red Mini-Minor, DFD 407C, complete with steam action!

Contents

Acknowledgements

In compiling this book I should like to thank the following people for all their help: Tricia Adams, Chris Banks, my wife Christina, Will Adams and all the team at Silver Link Publishing, and last but not least the BR staff who made it all possible.

Above Myself playing trumpet with Basil Kirchin and his band at the Strand Palais, Douglas, Isle of Man, in the summer of 1958. On stage, from left to right, are: Alan Randall (who went on to make a big name as a variety artist appearing in, amongst many others, the Royal Variety Command Performance), Basil Kirchin on drums, Ashley Kozak, Dave Davani, Johnny Marshall, myself, and vocalists Roy Landsford and Ricky James. During its time in the Isle of Man the band appeared on the legendary *Six-Five Special* TV programme, which was televised from the Villa Marina Gardens ballroom at the northern end of Douglas. The popularity of dance bands was such that at this time in Douglas there were four ballrooms, with well-known bands playing every evening in the summer season (and sometimes mornings and afternoons) to packed houses of dancers and listeners, as can be well seen in this picture.

Below left The Basil Kirchin band on tour in the United States, May 1958. From left to right in the foreground are vocalists Ricky James and Jilly Manners, myself and Basil Kirchin; behind are Johnny Marshall and Alan Randall.

Below The Basic Kirchin band coach (a Bedford?) on which I travelled throughout the country in 1958. This picture was taken at Dundee in June of that year during a week's tour of Scotland, taking in Edinburgh, Kilmarnock and Aberdeen as well as Dundee. Flanking the coach are Alan Randall (left) and Harry, the coach driver. Just imagine how many opportunities were missed to photograph steam during that week alone!

Introduction

It all started, or should I say re-started, in the late summer of 1965. I was on holiday at Exmouth in East Devon, and visited Bicton Gardens (situated just north of Budleigh Salterton), which among other attractions featured an 18-inch narrow gauge railway. Presumably for this reason the combined tea-rooms and book shop, as well as selling gardening books, also had what was for those days a wide range of railway books. While browsing through these, I came across a copy of Colin Gifford's now famous volume *Decline of Steam*, which had just been published. I suppose that like everyone else I had realised that steam power was being replaced on our railways, but a good read of this very fine book not only made me realise how quickly steam was going, but also re-awakened my interest in railways and railway photography.

In the late 1940s and early 1950s, while attending Halesowen Grammar School, the great interests in my life had been music, cricket and railways. I became a professional musician on leaving school at 17, first in the army and later as a peripatetic instrumental teacher. I have always followed cricket as much as I can and am a keen supporter of my local county team, Worcestershire. But as with a lot of people, my enthusiasm for railways became dormant while I pursued my career in music and girlfriends! That is, until that day in 1965 at Bicton Gardens.

We all regret things in life, lost opportunities and so on, but it was on that occasion that I realised that for around 12 years I had missed so much that was going on

in the railway world. As a musician I had travelled all over the United Kingdom as well as abroad during that period - I had been in the Army from 1954 to 1957, being in Germany most of the time - and had not taken one single railway picture. Just imagine - in 1958 I worked the summer season of eight weeks on the Isle of Man, when the island was bursting with steam routes, and I was free in the daytime. Similarly, I was in Newquay in the summer of 1960 for 17 weeks, playing at the exotically named Blue Lagoon Ballroom, when there was still plenty of steam activity in Cornwall.

In 1958, being based in London, I worked with well-known British band-leader Basil Kirchin (a former drummer with Ted Heath's band). We worked for three weeks in the United States during which time, and had I realised it I would have been able to see some of the wonderful American steam power still at work on the Norfolk & Western Railway based in Virginia. But these thoughts were all of what might have been, and the reality was that by the end of 1965 I was deciding that I must try to capture on film what was left of British steam before it all disappeared for ever.

By this time I was a regular subscriber to *Railway Magazine* and *Railway World*, so I had a reasonable idea of what was happening with regard to steam power. But, like most people when they embark on a new venture, I made mistakes. My principal one was that, from the last few weeks of 1965 through to the latter part of January 1966, I attempted to photograph steam with the camera

During the late 1940s and early 1950s, when I was actively train-spotting, like many other young lads I would often carry a camera around with me, but because of the cost of film and processing, etc, regrettably I did not take many pictures. Imagine seeing dozens of workings in a day, hauled by a rich variety of locomotives, and only taking two or three shots. Compare this to today, when people like myself will travel three, four, five hundred miles or even more, in pursuit of one steam special!

During the summer holidays (July/August) of 1950, I spent some time at Blakedown station near Kidderminster on the ex-GWR Snow Hill-Stourbridge Junction-Worcester route, this station being a short cycle ride from my home at Halesowen. Although this line was a secondary main line, in those days it was very busy with local trains, semi-fasts and much freight and coal traffic from South Wales to the factories of the Birmingham area and the Black Country. Local trains to and from Snow Hill called at Blakedown what seemed like every few minutes or so, especially in the morning and evening rush hours. In July 1950 I took this picture of ex-GWR 2-6-2 tank No 4118 as it paused at Blakedown with an early evening local for Kidderminster and Worcester.

This picture, also taken in the summer of 1950, shows the signalman and members of the PW staff at Blakedown. This signalman, whose name unfortunately I never knew, was a friendly character who, much to my delight, invited me into the box several times during my visits.

A view of the crossing gates and signal box at the western end of Blakedown station as an ex-GWR Prairie tank heads for Stourbridge Junction in August 1950.

In common with most small stations at that time, Blakedown had goods sidings, in this case situated on both sides of the main lines. During a day's spotting at Blakedown I would see a wide variety of GWR locomotives, including 'Castles' and what, at the time, were considered to be a fairly new GWR 4-6-0, the 'County' Class, which had only been introduced in 1945. The last one was No 1029, appropriately called *County of Worcester*, which was completed in April 1947. I saw 'Counties' a number of times on a regular working from Paddington to Worcester and Stourbridge Junction, which arrived at the latter location around 1 pm. After servicing at Stourbridge shed, it worked a local to Worcester Shrub Hill, then a tea-time express to Paddington. According to my spotting records of that time, No 1000 *County of Middlesex* was a regular performer on that working.

that I had used as a lad from the late 1940s to early in the 1950s. This was a Purma Special, taking 127 film with a fixed aperture and three shutter speeds, so the results were very hit-and-miss. So, with good advice from a friend and help from a local camera shop, I bought a new Konica 35 mm camera, which, coupled with Kodak Plus X film (rated at 125 ASA), produced very satisfactory results. My only regret is that I did not use any colour film until 1969, probably because at the time all the work in magazines and books was in black and white, which, as in *Decline of Steam*, seemed to suit the subject so well.

I was also fortunate in two other respects. For most of 1966, because of the nature of my profession, I had plenty of spare time during the day, as well as having my own transport in the shape of a Mini. During that year I clocked up around 30,000 miles in my quest for steam.

Looking back to 30 years ago, I realise that I was very lucky in being able to cover so much during the year, though not all of it by any means - I regret not seeing the

end of the Somerset & Dorset, for example. I count myself lucky to have seen so much in one year, and to have met so many friendly and helpful people amongst railwaymen and enthusiasts alike.

Although the present day can never be quite like the days of BR steam, it is wonderful to be able to still see steam on the main line and preserved lines, thanks to the army of enthusiasts who help to create this. So whether we photograph or ride on the trains, we can still get a good feel of the old days. Long may it continue!

January

THE HEADLINES. . .

1st   Bob Dylan is booed when he uses an electric guitar for the first time on his British tour.

12th   President Johnson delivers State of the Union message, including a report on the war in Vietnam, now in its third year.

15th   A Unilateral Declaration of Independence having been declared by Ian Smith's White-dominated government in 1965, further economic sanctions are introduced, including an oil embargo, by Britain.
Coup d'etat in Nigeria.

18th   A B52 bomber carrying four nuclear devices collides with a refuelling tanker - two bombs release plutonium, one falls intact, the other falls into sea and is recovered later (see April).

19th   Mrs Indira Gandhi is elected PM of India.

20th   Sir Robert Menzies retires as Australian PM.

27th   Labour wins the Hull by-election as expected. (Harold Wilson's Labour Government has been in power since 1964, and Barbara Castle is Minister of Transport.)

ENTERTAINMENT

At the cinema

Films released in the first three months of 1966 included *Alfie*, starring Michael Caine; *Morgan - A Suitable Case for Treatment*, an 'archetypal sixties marital fantasy' (Leslie Halliwell) starring David Warner; and *The Silencers*, the first of a series of 'James Bond'-type spoofs starring Dean Martin as Matt Helm: 'Follow his secret from bedroom to bedlam, with guns, girls and dynamite!' (publicity).

Television: Friday 28 January

BBC1
1.30 Watch with Mother: The Flowerpot Men; 4.45 Jackanory; 5.00 Crackerjack; 7.00 The Newcomers (new 'soap'); 7.30 The Vital Spark; 8.00 The Andy Williams Show; 8.50 News; 9.00 The Dick Van Dyke Show; 9.25 Tito Gobi introduces Great Characters in Opera; 10.05 24 Hours: What Matters Today; 10.40 Choice; 11.10 Weather and closedown

BBC2 highlights (since 1964)
7.30-11.05 mostly news, but including The Virginian and Wheelbase (later to become Top Gear, still popular 30 years later!)

ITV Rediffusion
4.45 Small Time; 5.00 Five O'Clock Club; 5.55 News; 6.07 Ready Steady Go! ('The weekend starts here!'); 6.35 Crossroads (introduced in 1964 as a daily serial); 7.00 Take Your Pick (with Michael Miles, more recently revived with Des O'Connor); 7.30 Emergency-Ward 10 (running since 1957); 8.00 The Avengers (with Diana Rigg as Emma Peel); 8.55 News; 9.10 Cinema; 9.40 A Man Called Shenandoah (western series starring Robert Horton); 10.05 Peyton Place; 10.35 News; 10.37 Late Show London - Benny Green and his guests; 11.17 What the Papers Say; 11.30 Dateline Westminster; Weather; 11.47 Dialogue with Doubt

Radio highlights

Home
1.30 The Archers; 1.45 Listen with Mother

Light
8.34 Housewives' Choice; 11.15 The Dales; 2.00 Woman's Hour

Chart entries

6th   Crispian St Peters, 'You Were On My Mind' (reached No 2)

13th   Cilla Black, 'Love's Just a Broken Heart' (No 5)
The Mindbenders, 'A Groovy Kind of Love' (No 2)
The Overlanders, 'Michelle' (No 1)
Pinkerton's Assorted Colours, 'Mirror Mirror' (No 9)
Sandie Shaw, 'Tomorrow' (No 9)
Nancy Sinatra, 'These Boots are Made for Walking' (No 1)

DECLINE OF STEAM. . .

Lines closed

3rd   Lancaster Castle to Green Ayre
Cheltenham Spa St James to Malvern Road
Morecambe (Promenade) to Wennington

23rd   Ryde Pierhead to Esplanade (opened again from 18 April to 18 September)

Stations closed

3rd   Adlestrop, Blockley Halt, Chipping Campden, Littleton & Badsey, Fladbury, Stoulton, Norton Halt (Kingham-Evesham, GW); Cheltenham Spa Malvern Road (GW); Grove Ferry & Upstreet (SEC); Middleton Junction (L&Y); Milcote Halt, Long Marston, Pebworth Halt (Stratford-Honeybourne, GW); Newton Heath (L&Y); Pebworth Halt (GW); Templecombe (Lower Platform) (S&D); Wyre Halt (GW)

31st   Hethersett (GE)

Loco sheds closed

3rd   Camden (1B), Annesley (16B)
16th   Hawick (64G)

Locomotives withdrawn

The last three Bulleid 'Q1' 0-6-0s, Nos 33006/20/27, were withdrawn on 9 January, and the last 'A3' 'Pacific', No 60052 *Prince Palatine*, on the 17th. Other withdrawals included 'BB' 'Pacific' No 34076 *41 Squadron*, 'Jubilee' 4-6-0 No 45643 *Rodney*, seven 'Black Five' 4-6-0s, 14 '8F' 2-8-0s, 15 'Austerity' 2-8-0s, and 21 Standard locos from six Classes, including '9F' 2-10-0s Nos 92068/72.

Total steam locos withdrawn in January: 104

Early January

Above right and right As I said in the introduction, as the start of 1966 I was still using the old Purma camera that I had used in the late 1940s, and it was not until towards the end of January that I purchased my new Konica 35 mm camera. These first two pictures, taken in early/mid-January 1966, were taken using the old equipment. The location is Stourbridge Junction station, looking towards Birmingham and Wolverhampton, the junction being just north of the station. The first shows ex-LMS '8F' 2-8-0 No 48531 (shedded at Stourbridge 2C) heading south with coal empties. Following in the same direction is 'Black Five' 4-6-0 No 44965 with a van train.

All the semaphore signals have long since gone, but the ex-GWR signal box is still there and in use. To the left of the box, but out of sight, is the line coming in from Stourbridge Town station, long the domain of the GWR '1400' Class 0-4-2 tank and auto-trailer, but now worked by a single DMU.

Monday 31 January

Armed with my new camera (purchased the previous Saturday) I head for Tyseley and, hopefully, quite a few steam pictures. Alas, by this time steam workings in the Birmingham area, except for specials, were confined to freight and parcels working, most of which ran 'Mondays excepted'. So I decided that to use my new camera, I would have to take a few diesel pictures. I hope that most of you will agree that even these are now of historical interest.

The first picture shows Brush Type 4 No 1853 approaching Tyseley station early in the afternoon, with the hourly Paddington-Snow Hill-Wolverhampton service. The North Warwickshire line from Stratford-upon-Avon is coming in from the right, and the whole scene is dominated by the fine array of semaphore signals and the GWR signal box in the centre of the picture.

In the second scene, taken shortly afterwards, two Brush Type 4s appeared, one unidentified, in charge of (right) an empty coaching stock (ECS) working from the Stratford line, probably heading for Tyseley carriage sidings, and a northbound mixed freight train; the latter is headed by No D1827.

The final scene shows another Type 4, No D1813, in two-tone green livery, heading for Tyseley carriage sidings with an ECS from the North Warwickshire line. By this time what light there had been was fading, so I decided to pack up for the day and return the following morning.

February

THE HEADLINES. . .

3rd   First 'soft' moon landing, by Soviet space probe *Luna IX*.

17th   Mark Bonham Carter, former Liberal MP, is appointed to chair the new Race Relations Board. The Labour Government appoints members of the Public Schools Commission to review the set-up of public schools and their integration into the state system.

20th   Chester Nimitz, US Admiral and Second World War Pacific Fleet Commander, dies.

21-24th   PM Harold Wilson is in Moscow for talks.

27th   The bulk of British troops are withdrawn from Libya (which was under British and French control until 1951), with the remainder leaving at the end of March. (Col Gaddafi was to seize control in a military coup in 1969.)

28th   Liverpool's Cavern Club, where Brian Epstein first saw local group The Beatles play, is forced into liquidation.

ENTERTAINMENT

Entrances and exits

1st   Buster Keaton dies at the age of 71.

1st   Hedda Hopper, former actress and later a powerful Hollywood columnist, dies from pneumonia at 76.

6th   Rick Astley born; hits include 'Never Gonna Give You Up' and 'Together Forever' in 1988.

10th   Laura Dern, daughter of actor Bruce, born; she will be in films from 1984, including *Blue Velvet* and *Wild at Heart*.

London theatres

Duke of York's: 'The Killing of Sister George' starring Beryl Reid
Globe: 'At the Drop of Another Hat', Flanders and Swann revue, featuring the song 'The Slow Train':
    'No more will I go to Blandford Forum and Mortehoe
    On the slow train from Midsomer Norton and Mumby Road. . .'

New production of Lionel Bart's 'Oliver' becomes the longest-running musical in history

Television: Saturday 12 February

BBC1
12.45-5.15 Sport; 5.15 Dr Who; 5.40 News and weather; 5.50 Juke Box Jury; 6.15 Dixon of Dock Green 7.00 Last of the Mohicans; 8.25 The Kathy Kirby Show; 9.10 Bewitched; 9.35 News and sport; 9.50 The Spies; 10.40 BBC3 (satirical show, successor to That Was The Week That Was); 11.40 Weather and closedown

BBC2 highlight
9.35 Not Only . . . But Also (Peter Cook and Dudley Moore)

ATV
Sport until 5.15 Thank Your Lucky Stars; 5.55 News; 6.00 Thunderbirds; 6.55 Bonanza; 7.50 The Enforcer (1950 Humphrey Bogart film); 9.20 Morecambe & Wise; 9.55 News; 10.05 Mystery and Imagination: The Fall of the House of Usher; 11.5 On the Braden Beat (consumer guidance show hosted by Bernard Braden with youthful assistant Esther Rantzen); 11.35 Interpol Calling (1959-vintage series); 12.00 Epilogue

Radio highlights

Home
1.10 The Men from the Ministry

Light
9.00 Children's Favourites

Chart entries

9th   Vince Hill, 'Edelweiss' (reached No 2)

10th   Petula Clark, 'My Love' (No 4)
The Rolling Stones, 'Nineteenth Nervous Breakdown' (No 2)
The Small Faces, 'Sha La La La Lee' (No 3)

17th   Eddy Arnold, 'Make the World Go Away' (No 8)
The Beach Boys, 'Barbara Ann, (No 3)
Gene Pitney, 'Backstage' (No 4)

24th   The Hollies, 'I Can't Let Go' (No 2)

DECLINE OF STEAM. . .

Lines closed

21st   Cowes to Ryde St John's Road
       Cowes to Newport
14th   Totton to Fawley
28th   Aberdeen (Ferryhill Junction) to Ballater

Stations closed

14th   Elderslie, Paisley West, Hawkhead, Shields Road, Cumberland Street (Paisley-Glasgow, GSW); Queensferry, Shotton Low Level, Connah's Quay, Bagillt, Holywell Junction, Mostyn, Talacre, Conway (re-opened as Conwy 29 June 1987), Menai Bridge, Gaerwen, Llanfair PG (re-opened 1970-72, and from 7 May 1973), Valley (re-opened 15 March 1982) (Chester-Holyhead, LNW); Draycott & Breaston, Borrowash (Trent-Derby, MR)
28th   Perth (Princes Street)

Loco sheds closed

6th   Langwith Junction (41J), Immingham (40B)
7th   Southampton Docks (70I)
14th   Fleetwood (10C), Lower Darwen (10H)
27th   Frodingham (36C) closed to steam, Percy Main (52E)
28th   Ballater (sub to Kittybrewster, 61A)

Locomotives withdrawn

'BB' 'Pacific' No 34079 *141 Squadron* was withdrawn on the 27th, and 'MN' No 35011 *General Steam Navigation* on the 6th. Other withdrawals included 12 '8F' 2-8-0s, 12 'B1' 4-6-0s, 30 'Austerity' 2-8-0s, and the last ex-GCR/ROD 'O4/3' 2-8-0, No 63764, from Leeds Neville Hill on the 27th.

Total steam locos withdrawn in February: 93
Cumulative total for year: 197

Tuesday 1 February
Back at Tyseley the next morning, the weather was still on the grey side, but there was some steam action to photograph. The first picture shows ex-LMS Ivatt Class '2MT' 2-6-0 No 46457 heading through the station for the North Warwickshire line with a load of coal wagons, and passing a fine selection of ex-GWR semaphore signals. The lines on the left-hand side lead to the shed and carriage sidings.

Tuesday 1 February
Looking in the opposite direction from the previous scene, I photographed BR Standard Class '9F' 2-10-0 No 92094 approaching Tyseley station with a northbound freight from the Paddington direction. Apart from a few ex-GWR pannier tanks and 'Castle' Class 4-6-0 No 7029, formerly *Clun Castle*, this area (now controlled by the London Midland Region) was worked by ex-LMS and Standard BR types of steam locomotives.

To complete this series of pictures, we see an unidentified Stanier '8F' 2-8-0 heading north with a mineral train, probably from the Banbury area, while on the right can be seen the rear of No 46457 returning after working down the North Warwickshire line.

Saturday 26 February

February was a very busy month for me, including playing with the Eric Delany Band in the 'Ovaltine' show at the Coventry Theatre. I was therefore unable to go out photographing again until this Saturday when, together with fellow musician and enthusiast, and a good friend of mine, Ken Blocksidge, I visited the Banbury and Oxford area. Ken, who sadly died in October 1971 (the weekend that steam returned to BR), was to accompany me on quite a few of my many trips in 1966.

Banbury shed, now 2D but formerly 84C in Western Region days, was once home to many GWR locomotives, but since passing into London Midland control, now played host to '8Fs', 'Black Fives' and BR Standard types. Here Class '5' 4-6-0 No 44860 receives a final grooming before it works out of Banbury with the York-Bournemouth train. On the left is sister loco No 45464. The shed was to close in October.

Peering out of the shed is '9F' 2-10-0 No 92013, which would be withdrawn from Saltley on 1 October after a life of only 12 years.

Saturday 26 February
This page Moving on to Oxford shed (81F), which had closed to steam a few weeks earlier at the end of 1965, when steam had been all but eliminated from the Western Region, we were greeted with a short spell of sunshine and several ex-GWR locomotives (all condemned but still with connecting rods, etc) in the shed yard.

The first picture shows Class '6100' '4MT' 2-6-2 tank No 6134. These powerful tank locomotives with their 5 ft 8 in driving wheels and tractive effort of 27,340 lbs were mainly used on the heavy Paddington suburban services.

In the second view 'Hall' Class 4-6-0 No 7919, formerly *Runter Hall*, is seen in line with No 6974, formerly *Helmingham Hall*.

An unidentified 'Hall' completes the trio of pictures.

Above right and right After our visit to what was left of Oxford shed we called in at the station just in time to see the arrival of the York-Bournemouth train, hauled by 4-6-0 No 44860, which we had seen earlier in Banbury shed yard. The train, complete with Southern coaches, is seen passing under the fine signal gantry at the north end of the station.

By now the weather was deteriorating rapidly, but we stayed just long enough to see No 44860 departing for the South Coast.

March

THE HEADLINES. . .

The UN is in Cyprus keeping the peace (since 1964). The grand total of all Government expenditure, Civil List, etc for 1966-67 is £6 billion (1994/5, £285.7 billion). During March to May natural gas is discovered in the North Sea and is beginning to be exploited.

1st   The unmanned Soviet *Venus 3* spacecraft touches down on Venus.

10th   Parliament is dissolved before the election. The wedding of Princess Beatrix of the Netherlands to a West German diplomat (Queen from 1980).

20th   Football World Cup is stolen from Central Hall, Westminster, but is recovered one week later.

22-24th   The Archbishop of Canterbury, Dr Michael Ramsey, visits Pope Paul VI at the Vatican.

26th   The University Boat Race is won by Oxford by 3¾ lengths.

31st   General Election. Harold Wilson's Labour Government is returned with a majority of 97.

ENTERTAINMENT

London theatres

Drury Lane: 'Hello Dolly' with Mary Martin
Mayfair: 'Beyond the Fringe', successor to the original influential production that opened in Edinburgh in 1960

Television: Tuesday 22 March

BBC1
4.45 Jackanory; 5.00 Hiram Holliday; 5.25 Tom Tom; 5.50 Peter's Adventure; 5.55 News; 6.05 Town and Around; 6.30 Catch me a Colobus
7.00 The Newcomers; 7.30 Frankie Howerd; 8.00 Miss Sadie Thompson (1953 film starring Rita Hayworth); 8.50 News; 9.10 Labour Party Election Broadcast; 9.20 Film part 2; 9.55 Sportsview (which ran from 1954-1970 fronted by Peter Dimmock); 10.30 24 Hours (thrice-weekly from the mid-'60s to mid'70s, fronted by Cliff Michelmore, Kenneth Allsop, Ludovic Kennedy, etc); 11.10 Bonjour Francoise; 11.35 Weather and close-down

BBC2 highlight
9.20 Show of the Week presented by Vikki Carr

ITV Rediffusion
4.45 Small Time; 5.00 Five O'Clock Club; 5.25 Object 2 Returns (serial); 5.55 News; 6.07 The Addams Family; 6.35 Crossroads
7.00 Double your Money with Hughie Green; 7.30 Emergency-Ward 10; 8.00 Mrs Thursday, starring Kathleen Harrison; 8.55 News; 9.10 Labour Party Election Broadcast; 9.20 Amos Burke: Secret Agent (successor to Burke's Law starring Gene Barry); 10.18 TV and the General Election; 10.50 Election 66; 11.10 The Reporter, series starring Harry Guardino; 12.05 Change of Heart

Radio highlights

Home
12.25 Round Britain Quiz (still popular in 1996)

Light
10.31 Music While You Work; 12.15 Midday Spin; 1.00 Pop Inn

Chart entries

3rd   Dave Dee, Dozy, Beaky, Mick and Tich, 'Hold Tight' (reached No 4)
The Kinks, 'Dedicated Follower of Fashion' (No 4)
The Walker Brothers, 'The Sun Ain't Gonna Shine Any More' (No 1)
The Yardbirds, 'Shapes of Things' (No 3)

10th   Bob Lind, 'Elusive Butterfly' (No 5)
The Who, 'Substitute, (No 5)

17th   The Bachelors, 'The Sound of Silence' (No 3)
Val Doonican, 'Elusive Butterfly' (No 5)

24th   The Spencer Davis Group, 'Somebody Help Me' (No 1)
Simon & Garfunkel, 'Homeward Bound' (No 9)

31st   Dusty Springfield, 'You Don't Have To Say You Love Me' (No 1)
Crispian St Peters, 'Pied Piper' (No 5)
Cilla Black, 'Alfie' (No 9)
Cher, 'Bang Bang' (No 3)
Alan Price, 'I Put a Spell on You' (No 10)

DECLINE OF STEAM. . .

Closure of the S&D on the 7th eliminated steam from the Western Region, and by the 27th all the 36 remaining Eastern Region steam locomotives (seven 'B1s', five '04/8s', 19 'WD' 2-8-0s and five '9Fs') were allocated to one depot, Doncaster (36A).

Lines closed

7th   Seaton Junction to Seaton
        Bath Green Park to Mangotsfield (inc)
        Bath Green Park to Broadstone and Poole (Holes Bay Junction)
        Evercreech Junction to Highbridge and Burnham on Sea
        Christ's Hospital (Itchingfield Junction) to Shoreham-by-Sea
        Stranraer Town to Harbour Junction
28th   Connel Ferry to Ballachulish

Stations closed

7th   Coldham (GE); Staple Hill, Fishponds (Mangotsfield-Bristol, MR); Wilton South, Dinton, Semley, Templecombe (re-opened 3 October 1983), Milborne Port Halt, Chard Junction, Seaton Junction, Broadclyst, Pinhoe (Salisbury-Exeter, LSW)

Loco sheds closed

7th   Bath Green Park (82F) and Templecombe (83G), together with sub-sheds at Radstock and Highbridge.
27th   Darlington steam shed (51A)
28th   Ballachulish (sub-shed to Oban, 63C)
        Bescot (2F) (diesel depot not yet built)

Locomotives withdrawn

Two '5700' 0-6-0PTs, Nos 3681 and 3758, three '8Fs', Nos 48309/706/760 (of the 16 withdrawn this month), and two LMS 0-6-0Ts, Nos 47276 and 47506, were withdrawn from Bath Green Park when it closed. Also withdrawn during the month were 'WC' 'Pacific' No 34048 *Crediton* on the 13th, 'Jubilee' No 45574 *India* on the 20th, and 'Britannia' No 70019 *Lightning* on the 12th.

Total steam locos withdrawn in March: 77
Cumulative total for year: 274

Saturday 12 March
Although my local station, Halesowen, had been closed (apart from Austin workmen's trains) to passenger traffic in 1927, there were still regular freight workings to and from the Birmingham and Stourbridge areas, right until 1969 when Halesowen Canal Basin closed. All these trains now ran via Old Hill on the Snow Hill-Stourbridge Junction route, because the section of the through route from Longbridge (on the LMS Birmingham-Bristol main line) to Halesowen and on to Old Hill (GWR) had been closed between Longbridge and Halesowen in 1963. This line was originally a joint line between the Midland Railway and the GWR, opened in 1883. I well remember in the late 1940s seeing ex-Midland Railway Class '2F' 0-6-0s (designed by Johnson and originally built in 1875) working over the branch from Longbridge.
    The first of three scenes at Halesowen shows pannier tank No 8718 taking water in the Longbridge side of Halesowen station - the line terminated just around the corner. This locomotive had only a few months to go before withdrawal from Shrewsbury shed on 23 July.

Saturday 12 March

Ex-GWR 0-6-0 pannier tank No 4635 pauses between shunting duties, then Nos 4635 and 8718 are seen prior to leaving and taking out the afternoon goods to either the Stourbridge or Birmingham areas. To my knowl-edge, a banking locomotive was always required for the steep climb between Halesowen and Old Hill. No 4635 was also withdrawn in July, on the 16th from Tyseley shed.

Sunday 13 March

The next day saw me paying a visit to Stourbridge shed (originally 84F but now 2C). The shed was situated on the west side of the Wolverhampton line, north of Stourbridge Junction station.

It was a very dull day, but grimy '8F' 2-8-0 No 48121 does its best to brighten things up. Just visible in the murky background is Standard Class '5MT' 4-6-0 No 73026. Also on the shed that day were Class '2MT' 2-6-0s Nos 46427 and 46492, pannier tanks Nos 3607, 9614, 9641 and 9724, and another '8F', No 48550.

Saturday 19 March

'8F' 2-8-0 No 48417 heads through Brettell Lane with a goods train for Dudley; the container is worthy of note, boasting the 'door-to-door' service on its side.

This location, situated between Stourbridge Junction and Brierley Hill, was the junction for the line to Wombourne and Wolverhampton, which can be seen clearly swinging away to the left past the signal box. This line, which had closed to traffic in 1965, joined the Wolverhampton to Shrewsbury line at Oxley, a mile or so north of Wolverhampton Low Level station, thus forming an avoiding line for that town.

Saturday 19 March
0-6-0 pannier tank No 3718 heads through Lyde Green, near Lye on the Birmingham-Stourbridge Junction route, with a train of empties bound for the Stourbridge area. Note the shovel on the back of the bunker.

Sunday 20 March
By early 1966 control of the former GCR line from Marylebone to Nottingham and the North Midlands had passed from the Eastern Region of BR to the London Midland Region. A visit to the old GCR shed at Colwick (Nottingham) bore evidence to this, because all the ex-LNER locomotives were awaiting scrapping in the shed yard, and the shed was full of 'Black Fives', '8Fs' and Standard locomotives. The shed itself was to close to steam altogether in December.

Awaiting its fate in Colwick shed yard was ex-LNER Class 'B1' 4-6-0 No 61281, which had been withdrawn a few weeks earlier on 19 February. These fine mixed-traffic locomotives, designed by Thompson and built in the early 1940s, were once the mainstay of the LNER, numbering nearly 400 in their heyday. Beyond are 2-8-0s Nos 63816 and 63675, with had been taken out of service on 15 January.

A close-up of No 63675 with ex-'WD' Class 2-8-0 No 90606 at the rear, also recently out of use. Nos 63675 and 63816 were very powerful Class 'O4' freight locomotives, built to a design by Robinson of the GCR, with a tractive effort of 31,315 lbs, and ideal for hauling the heavy coal and freight trains of the industrial East and North Midlands.

The intruders take over! Colwick shed now plays host to '8F' No 48258, 'Black Five' No 44811, '8F' No 48137 and Standard Class '4MT' 2-6-0 No 76089.

Apparently Colwick was a difficult shed to get round, and when I turned up on that Sunday (without a pass) I was turned away. However, fortunately for me, at that moment a coachload of number-spotters were just getting off their coach for a visit to the shed (they were probably doing at least a dozen sheds in a day!) and I was able to join on to the back of them and wander round the shed.

Tuesday 29 March

Towards the end of the month Ken Blocksidge and myself decided to spend a week in the North of England, photographing as much steam as possible. The 29th saw us at Scout Green, just over halfway up on the notorious Shap incline (5 miles at 1 in 75) between Tebay to the south and Shap summit.

These days the electrics fly up the bank, but in steam days a lot of trains needed banking assistance, usually in the form of ex-LMS 2-6-4 tank engines. One of the first pictures that I took on that spring day was of 2-6-4T No 42154 pausing at Scout Green box (on its way back to Tebay after assisting a northbound goods) to give a lift to a railwayman. Could this be the ideal way to travel home after work?

Less than an hour later No 42154 was in action again, banking the 10.35 am Euston-Carlisle train (hauled by 'Britannia' 'Pacific' No 70013, formerly *Oliver Cromwell*).

Two views of 'Black Five' 4-6-0 No 45326 as it climbs Shap with an afternoon Crewe-Carlisle parcels train, first approaching Scout Green, and the 'going away' shot as it is about to pass the famous box.

The signalman on duty was very friendly and invited us into the box, giving us details of many freight workings and also advising us where to stay in the small railway town of Tebay.

Wednesday 30 March

Above The next day, after having spent a very comfortable night in an excellent pub in the centre of Tebay (the Cross Keys Inn), we decided to spend some time around Tebay before heading for Carlisle. Tebay shed (12E) was situated on the western side of the main line and permission was soon granted by the station staff for a look round.

The first scene, looking out of the shed, shows Fairburn 2-6-4T No 42225 just outside, with the previous day's No 42154 at the coaling tower. No 42225 lasted only until 18 June before it was withdrawn.

Left Looking back into the shed we see, from left to right, 2-6-4T No 42210, Class '4MT' 2-6-0s Nos 43033 and 43035, and on the extreme right, another unidentified member of the same class. Unseen behind No 42210 is 2-6-4T No 42232.

After visiting the shed we went back to Tebay station, but as can be seen from this picture of 'Britannia' 'Pacific' No 70040 (formerly *Clive of India*) on a southbound parcels train, the weather was deteriorating, so we drove on to Carlisle.

The architecture of the former LNWR station is worthy of note. Also, in the distance just to the right of the locomotive can be seen the top of a brake-van, which is parked on the former NER line to Kirkby Stephen, Barnard Castle and Darlington (via Stainmore summit). This route closed in the early 1960s.

On arrival in Carlisle we went straight to Citadel station, where, parked in one of the middle roads and receiving a perhaps critical glance from a driver or fireman, was another 'Britannia', No 70046 (formerly *Anzac*). By this time nearly all the members of this famous class had had their names removed. It is nice to know that No 70000 *Britannia* herself is still in action on the main line today!

Wednesday 30 March

Left Ex-LMS Ivatt Class '2MT' 2-6-2T No 41217 shunting GPO vans at the northern end of Carlisle Citadel station. The station lost part of its magnificent roof in the late 1940s, but as can be seen in this and the previous picture, the walls still remain.

In the bay platform in the background, an early DMU waits to leave with a branch train, probably to Silloth.

Thursday 31 March

Below left After staying overnight in Carlisle, we spent the morning of General Election day around the Kingmoor area. The first photograph I took was of 'Black Five' 4-6-0 No 44903 heading out of Carlisle with a northbound goods, crossing the River Eden just south of the Kingmoor shed area.

This page Although we were refused permission to look round Kingmoor shed (12A), the walk to and from the shed master's office enabled us to take a few pictures in the shed yard.

The first picture shows the last rebuilt 'Patriot' Class 4-6-0, No 45530 *Sir Frank Ree*, awaiting its fate. These handsome locomotives were rebuilt by Ivatt in 1946 from the original Fowler 'Patriot' Class, introduced in 1933.

The second photograph shows rebuilt 'Royal Scot' Class 4-6-0 No 46115 *Scots Guardsman*, which, happily, is preserved. 'Jinty' Class '3F' 0-6-0T No 47531 stands behind.

Completing these Kingmoor shed scenes is 'Britannia' 'Pacific' No 70016 (formerly *Ariel*) coupled to an unidentified 'Black Five'. On the extreme right, below the shed clock, is Standard Class '9F' 2-10-0 No 92069. Even by this date Kingmoor shed had a fair number of steam locomotives on its books. At one time Carlisle boasted three main sheds, but Carlisle Canal was closed in 1963, and Upperby was closed to steam at the end of 1966.

Thursday 31 March

Left Before leaving the Carlisle area and travelling across the Pennines to Newcastle, we were able to photograph 'Black Five' 4-6-0 No 44879 as it passed the west side of Kingmoor shed and headed down the West Coast Main Line with a northbound tank train.

Below left A few minutes later, BR Standard Class '9F' 2-10-0 No 92017 pulled round the Carlisle avoiding line with a mixed freight train. This line, which comes off the WCML at Upperby (just south of Carlisle station), rejoins the main line at Caldew Junction, just north of Kingmoor.

By the time we had driven to Newcastle it was mid-afternoon, but we did manage to photograph former North Eastern (ex-LNER Class 'J27') 0-6-0 No 65788 as it headed past Gateshead Locomotive Depot (52A) with an empty mineral train. This class of locomotives, which were introduced in 1906, ran until the autumn of 1967, when steam finished in the Newcastle area. No 65788 lasted only until 5 June, when it was withdrawn from Sunderland.

We then drove south to Darlington for an overnight stop, staying up to follow the General Election results on the TV, the election giving a comfortable victory for Harold Wilson and the Labour Party.

April

THE HEADLINES. . .

Failure of 1965-66 crop in India leads to a food crisis - foreign aid is sent.
Increasing international ramifications of the Vietnam War.

7th   A US hydrogen bomb is recovered after 13 weeks in the sea off the Spanish Mediterranean coast.

19th   4,500 Australians join US forces in Vietnam.

21st   The new Parliament opens.

ENTERTAINMENT

Entrances and exits

2nd   C. S. Forester, author of the Hornblower novels, dies
10th   Evelyn Waugh, novelist, dies
15th   Samantha Fox born, topless model who went on to have a series of hits in 1987-8 including 'Nothing's Gonna Stop Me Now'

At the cinema

On 9 April Sophia Loren married Carlo Ponti in Paris (he was still married to his Italian wife under Italian law).
  On the 18th the Academy Awards Ceremony was MC'd by Bob Hope, who received a special gold medal for 'unique and distinguished service to our industry and the Academy'. *The Sound of Music* and *Dr Zhivago*, both nominated for 10 awards, won five each. Best Picture was *The Sound of Music*, Best Actor was Lee Marvin in *Cat Ballou*, Best Actress was Julie Christie in *Darling*, and Best Director was Robert Wise for *The Sound of Music*.

London theatres

Apollo: 'Spring and Port Wine' starring Alfred Marks
Ambassadors: 'The Mousetrap' in its 14th year (the world's longest ever run, in its 44th year in 1996 at St Martins Theatre)

Television: Monday 4 April

BBC1
4.45 Jackanory; 5.00 Blue Peter; 5.25 The Tich and Quackers Show; 5.50 Adventures of Tin Tin; 5.55 News; 6.5 Town and Around; 6.30 The White Heather Club (which introduced Moira Anderson to TV) 7.00 United! (serial); 7.30 Hugh and I (comedy with Hugh Lloyd and Terry Scott); 8.00 Panorama (on Monday nights since 1953, and still so); 8.50 News; 9.00 Perry Mason; 9.50 24 Hours; 10.30 Dance Date at the Lyceum, London; 11.10 Preacher and Poet; 11.20 Weather and closedown

BBC2 highlights
8.00 The Danny Kaye Show; 9.50 30 Minute Theatre: A Girl's Best Friend (a series of plays, originally live and thus now lost, running until 1972 and featuring early works by Dennis Potter and Tom Stoppard, and Alec Guinness's first British TV appearance)

ITV Rediffusion
4.45 Small Time; 5.00 Action; 5.25 Flipper (last year of the boy-and-dolphin series); 5.55 News; 6.07 Criss Cross Quiz (host Jeremy Hawk); 6.35 Crossroads 7.00 All Our Yesterdays (1960-73, presented by Brian Inglis); 7.30 Coronation Street; 8 The Rat Catchers, spy series starring Gerald Flood and Glyn Owen; 8.55 News; 9.10 A Man Called Shenandoah; 9.40 Play of the Week: A View from the Bridge by Arthur Miller; 11.23 News; 11.25 Dateline; 11.35 Holy Week

Radio highlights

Light
11.31 Monday Melody Time; 7.31 Benny Hill Time; 10.00 I'm Sorry I'll Read That Again ('The Wonder Show of BBC Radio', an influential pre-Python teaming of Tim Brooke-Taylor, John Cleese, Graeme Garden, David Hatch, Jo Kendall and Bill Oddie - remember the 'Angus Prune Tune'?)

Chart entries

14th   The Lovin' Spoonful, 'Daydream' (reached No 2)
21st   The Beach Boys, 'Sloop John B' (No 2)
        Roy C, 'Shotgun Wedding' (No 6)
        Manfred Mann, 'Pretty Flamingo' (No 2)

DECLINE OF STEAM. . .

The remaining steam locomotive withdrawals from Doncaster (36A) eliminated steam on the Eastern Region, except for nine ex-LMS tank locos, Nos 41528/533, 41708/34/63/804/835 and 47001/5, which were used as shunters at Staveley and could not be condemned until an 1866 legal agreement between the Midland Railway and Staveley Works had been repealed. Nominally allocated to Langwith Junction (41J), which had closed in February, they were actually stored at Canklow.

Lines closed

18th   Gorbals to Strathbungo Junction, Glasgow
Royton Junction to Royton
Keswick to Workington (Derwent Junction)
Wyre Dock to Fleetwood
Patney & Chirton to Holt Junction
Ventnor to Shanklin

Stations closed

18th   Beeston Castle & Tarporley, Tattenhall Road (Crewe-Chester, LNW); Blackwell, Stoke Works (Birmingham-Cheltenham, MR/GW); Boscarne Exchange Platform (GW); Corby, Gretton (Kettering-Manton Junction, MR); Crosshouse (GSW); Greenhill (CR); Harburn, Cobbinshaw, Auchengray, Carnwath (Edinburgh-Carstairs, CR); Old Dalby (MR); Oldham Central (L&Y);

Staverton Halt, Holt Junction, Lacock Halt (Trowbridge-Chippenham, GW); Savernake, Wootton Rivers Halt, Manningford Halt, Woodborough, Patney & Chirton, Lavington (GW); Milliken Park (GSW)

Loco sheds closed

17th   Doncaster (36A) closed to steam
18th   Mold Junction (6B), Lancaster (10J)

Locomotives withdrawn

Amongst this month's withdrawals were 'BB' 'Pacific' No 34082 *615 Squadron* on the 24th, 'WC' 'Pacific' No 34097 *Holsworthy* on the 10th, Standard 'Clan' 'Pacific' No 72008 *Clan Macleod* on the 16th and the last four Class 'O4/8' 2-8-0s Nos 63653/781/818/858 (all at Doncaster). Eight ex-LMS 'Jinties', ten '8Fs', nine 'B1s', 18 'Austerity' 2-8-0s (also all from Doncaster), and five '9Fs' were also withdrawn.

Total steam locos withdrawn in April: 79
Cumulative total for year: 353

Friday 1 April
Leaving Newcastle, we went to Darlington shed (51A), where we were given permission to look round. The shed had closed to steam a few days before, but several locomotives were stored there, including the last two ex-

LNER 'A1' 'Pacific' locomotives, both of which had been in steam on 26 March, the day the shed closed to steam. The first view shows No 60124 (formerly *Kenilworth*) and, just beyond, the rear of former NER 0-6-0 (ex-LNER 'J21' Class) No 65033, now preserved.

Friday 1 April
Above The last 'A1' 'Pacific' in service, No 60145 *Saint Mungo*, which was to be withdrawn from York on 19 June. All the members of this fine class of express locomotives were scrapped, but happily, thanks to the efforts of the North Eastern Locomotive Preservation Group (NELPG), a brand new 'A1' locomotive is being built.

As well as a 'WD' 2-8-0 and a 'Black Five' 4-6-0, stored inside the shed was 'A4' 'Pacific' No 60010 *Dominion of Canada*, now preserved in that country.

Below After visiting Darlington shed we went to the station, where on show are two original Stockton & Darlington locomotives: 0-4-0 *Locomotion*, built by Robert Stephenson and used for the opening of the line in 1825, and 0-6-0 *Derwent*, built for the line in 1845.

Unfortunately, the Darlington area was now virtually steamless, so we drove south to York. By this time it was beginning to sleet, so we decided to visit the Railway Museum, which in those days was housed in a shed at the southern end of the station. This view shows GNR Ivatt 4-4-2 No 990 *Henry Oakley*, built in 1898, and just beyond the 'Atlantic' is NER Class 'M1' 4-4-0 No 1621, built by Worsdell in 1893.

On leaving the museum we made a quick visit to York shed yard, but the weather was still bad, so we decided to head for Leeds (hoping to return to the York area in the near future) for our overnight stay.

Saturday 2 April
Opposite page Moving on to Leeds enabled us to visit the old Central station. We had been told that it was due for closure in the near future (in the event it was to last until 1 May 1967), and that the shunting duties at the station were carried out by ex-LMS Fairburn 2-6-4 tank locomotives. We were not disappointed, and overnight it had snowed, giving us the chance of photographing steam in the snow. After digging out the car, we arrived at Central station around mid-morning, where there was a fair amount of steam activity.

These two pictures show 2-6-4T No 42689 and a brake-van shunting the ECS of a King's Cross-Leeds express, and waiting to leave the ex-LNER station, having completed its shunting work. Note the LNER-type signals.

Saturday 2 April
It is snowing again as another ex-LMS 2-6-4T, this time No 42073, shunts vans at Leeds Central.

By 1966, steam had long finished on the Leeds-King's Cross service, to be replaced by (dare one say it!) the very popular English Electric 'Deltic' Class diesel locomotive. No D9015 *Tulyar* of that class waits at Central station after bringing in a train from King's Cross. *Tulyar* lasted until the very end of 'Deltic' operation in January 1982, and is now preserved.

After visiting Central station, we went across to Leeds City station where, on one of the outside tracks, Class 'Q6' 0-8-0 No 63340 (built by Raven for the NER in 1913) poses in the snow with a train of flat wagons.

It was amazing that in 1966 there were so many pre-Grouping locomotives still to be seen in the North East of England as well as Scotland and, of course, the Isle of Wight, as we shall see later. No 63440 was withdrawn on the last day of 1966.

There were still several sheds playing host to steam in the Leeds and West Riding area at this time, and on that Saturday, having failed to get a look round 55A Holbeck (without a pass, I hasten to add), we drove on to 55C Farnley Junction shed (situated south-west of Leeds on the line to Morley), where permission was given for a look round. On shed that day, with wintry shafts of sunlight coming through the leaky shed roof, was ex-LMS 'Jubilee' Class 4-6-0 No 45581 (formerly *Bihar & Orissa*), one of the last of this famous class of express locomotives still in service, and withdrawn on 7 August.

Also on shed that day were 'Black Fives' Nos 44729, 44826 and 45428, '8F' No 48080, and ex-'WDs' Nos 90254 and 90649. The shed was to close in November.

We decided to stay at Wakefield overnight before travelling back to Birmingham the following day. Late that Saturday afternoon saw us at Wakefield shed (56A), where I was able to photograph ex-LNER Class 'B1' 4-6-0 No 61013.

Sunday 3 April

Above Next morning we headed back to Birmingham, calling in at Royston shed (55D) on the way. On parade outside the shed were, from right to left, '8Fs' Nos 48710 and 48113, 2-6-0s Nos 43078 and 43076, 'WD' 2-8-0 No 90707, an unidentified '8F', 8F No 48067, and, just visible on the extreme left, 'Black Five' No 44912. This provided a fitting end to a very enjoyable few days in the North of England. As we will see, I was lucky enough to be able to visit most of these areas again later in the year.

Maundy Thursday, 7 April

Below Within a few days I was out photographing steam again, and decided to spend a couple of days in the South of England, where there was still a fair amount of activity on the Southern main line to Southampton and Bournemouth.

On my way to the Basingstoke area, I called first at Salisbury where, although steam from Waterloo to Exeter had finished a few months earlier, Salisbury shed (70E) still had an allocation of steam, and there were still a few steam workings, mainly on parcels and goods trains, and as replacements for diesel failures.

Early on that wet Thursday morning I was at Salisbury's fine old station in time to see a grimy Standard Class '4MT' 2-6-0 No 76067 on an up parcels train. As the locomotive was shedded at Bournemouth (70F) at the time, it was probably heading for either there or Southampton.

Above Shortly afterwards I paid a visit to Salisbury shed, which was on the south side of the main line to Exeter and just west of the station; it was famous for the cleanliness of its locomotives. Inside the shed Standard Class '4MT' 4-6-0 No 75068 catches the light from the shed doorway. On the right is 2-6-0 No 76007.

Below Also on shed that morning was 'West Country' 'Pacific' No 34015 *Exmouth* side by side with 'Battle of Britain' 4-6-2 No 34055 *Spitfire*. The latter did not last out the year, being withdrawn from Salisbury in September.

Thursday 7 April

Above I arrived at a wet Basingstoke station in the afternoon just in time to see Class '5' 4-6-0 No 44872 (of Banbury shed) taking water prior to leaving with the York to Bournemouth train. The fireman has cigarette in mouth - it's amazing how many people (myself included) smoked in those days. For most people it was probably a hangover from the war and National Service, which only finished in 1962.

Below A grey-looking locomotive for an equally grey day. 'Battle of Britain' 4-6-2 No 34060 25 *Squadron* approaches the eastern end of Basingstoke with a down Bournemouth service.

Above 'Battle of Britain' 4-6-2 No 34064 *Fighter Command*, probably deputising for a diesel, pulls out of Basingstoke with a train for Salisbury and approaches one of the splendid SR signal gantries that Basingstoke possessed. Note also the SR-style platform lamp on the extreme right. The locomotive had only a few more weeks of service left, being withdrawn on 22 May.

Below A short while after No 34064 departed, 'Merchant Navy' 'Pacific' No 35050 *Elder Dempster Lines* sped through the station with an afternoon Waterloo-Bournemouth train.

Good Friday, 8 April

The next morning dawned clear and bright and I was able to spend some time at the lineside at Basing (to the east of Basingstoke) before returning to the Midlands.

Standard Class '5MT' 4-6-0 No 73169 heads up the former LSWR four-track main line with a morning semi-fast bound for Waterloo, to be followed a few minutes later by Bulleid 'Battle of Britain' 'Pacific' No 34082 615 *Squadron* in charge of a down Bournemouth express. Only a couple of weeks later, on the 24th, No 34082 was taken out of service at Eastleigh.

Because it was Good Friday, BR was running to a Sunday timetable. I remember there being quite a gap before the next train, which was a down express hauled by 'West Country' 4-6-2 No 34034 *Honiton*.

It was beginning to cloud over when I took my final picture of an up Southampton boat train hauled by another 'West Country' 'Pacific', this time No 34037 *Clovelly*. The Southern coaches look immaculate - in contrast to the locomotive!

Saturday 23 April

Above I was busy for the next two weeks, and apart from a short visit to the Banbury area where the weather was atrocious, the next pictures I took were at Shrewsbury station. Standard Class '4MT' 4-6-0 No 75012 is shown waiting to leave Shrewsbury with the down 'Cambrian Coast Express'. The GWR 'Manor' Class 4-6-0s (which had previously worked these trains) were now out of service and the Standard 4-6-0s had taken over at the beginning of 1966. They continued to work this service until March 1967, when the through train from Paddington finished.

Sunday 24 April

Left The following day Ken Blocksidge and myself visited Crewe South shed (5B), where there was a variety of locomotives including this Class '5MT' 'Crab' 2-6-0 No 42727, seen basking in the late afternoon sunshine alongside '9F' 2-10-0 No 92037. On the left-hand side is BR Standard Class '4MT' 2-6-0 No 76040, and beyond the 'Crab' an unidentified 'Black Five'.

The powerful mixed-traffic 'Crab' 2-6-0s were first introduced in 1926 and, being designed by Hughes (built under Fowler's direction), owe their origins to the Lancashire & Yorkshire Railway.

Opposite page A short journey south from Crewe brought us to Stoke shed (5D) where the late evening sunshine highlighted (*above*) 4-6-0 No 45060 as it stood by the coaling plant, and two '9F' 2-10-0s, Nos 92101 and 92102 (*below*).

Saturday 30 April

Above The Ffestiniog Railway Society ran a special train from Paddington to Portmadoc, seen here hauled by Class '5' 4-6-0 No 44872 as it leaves Birmingham Snow Hill station for Shrewsbury and the Cambrian line to Machynlleth and Portmadoc.

Looking at this picture now makes one realise what a fine-looking station Snow Hill was, with its lengthy and spacious platforms. I have the most happy memories of this wonderful station, having started my train-spotting

days there in 1948. It closed from 6 March 1972, although a smaller station on the same site was later re-instated.

Below Shortly after the special had passed through Snow hill, a pair of freights came through. On the left, '8F' 2-8-0 No 48550 heads in the Wolverhampton direction, as Class '5' 4-6-0 No 45263 pulls up the bank from Hockley with a southbound goods.

Above From a chance conversation at Snow Hill while waiting for the Ffestiniog special, I found out that an ex-LNER Class 'K1' 2-6-0 had worked into Burton-on-Trent from York that morning. So after I finished photographing at Snow Hill, I drove over to Burton where on the shed, resplendent in the afternoon sunshine, was No 62012 (of York shed, 50A). Burton shed (17B), with its Midland Railway ancestry, must have been one of the finest designs in the country.

Below A look inside Burton shed on that Saturday afternoon revealed '8F' No 48254 and Midland Railway-design 'Jinty' 0-6-0T No 47643. On the left is the rear of '8F' No 48700, and an '03' Class diesel shunter is on the right-hand side.

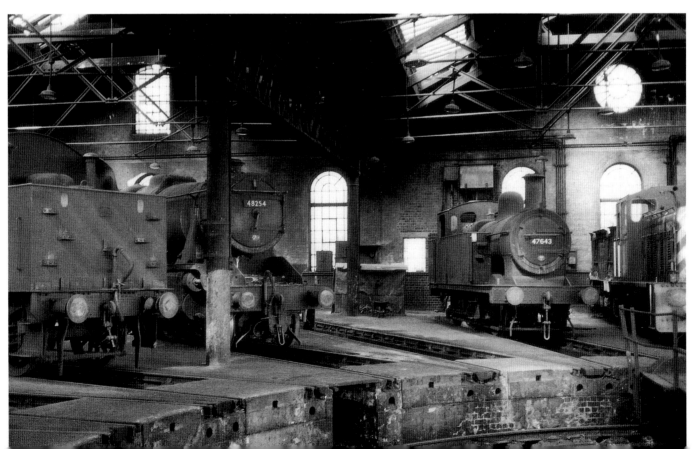

May

THE HEADLINES. . .

The Football League Championship is won by Liverpool.

5th   It is reported that the purchasing power of £1 has been halved in the past 20 years.

6th   Moors murderers Ian Brady and Myra Hindley are sentenced to three and two life sentences respectively for the murders of several children.

13th   A project is initiated to look at the preservation of historic cities - Bath, York, Chester, King's Lynn and Chichester.

14th   The FA Cup is won by Everton.

21st   Prohibition is repealed in Mississippi - liquor may be sold from 1 July.
Cassius Clay beats Henry Cooper in Round 6 of the World Heavyweight Championship.

24th   A plan is announced for 'polytechnics' - about 30 initially, with ultimate growth to 2,000 students. There is also talk of a University of the Air (which was to become the Open University in 1969, with courses starting in 1971).

25th   Women are admitted as elders in the Church of Scotland.

26th   British Guiana becomes independent within the Commonwealth.
Zola Budd is born. She caused controversy in 1984 when she obtained British citizenship and was selected for the British Olympic squad. She set the world record for the 5,000 metres in 1984 and 1985, and retired in 1988.

ENTERTAINMENT

Entrance

26th   Helena Bonham Carter born, later featuring in several costume films including *A Room With A View* (1985) and *Howards End* (1992).

At the cinema

Blue Max (the story of German First World War flying aces, starring George Peppard and James Mason) is one of the biggest pictures of the summer. The film of comic-strip character *Modesty Blaise*, starring Monica Vitti, is directed by Joseph Losey, and *The Wild Angels* - Roger Corman's violent biker film starring Peter Fonda, Nancy Sinatra and Bruce Dern, is banned in Britain.

London theatres

Adelphi: 'Charlie Girl' starring Joe Brown and Anna Neagle
Drury Lane: 'Hello Dolly' - Dora Bryan takes over
Palladium: 'London Laughs' with Harry Secombe, Jimmy Tarbuck, Thora Hird, Freddie Frinton, Anita Harris and Russ Conway

Television: Wednesday 25 May

BBC1
2.25-3.45 Derby Day Grandstand; 4.45 Jackanory; 5.00 Champion the Wonder Horse (already ten years old at this time); 5.25 Animal Magic with Johnny Morris; 5.50 Adventures of Tin Tin; 6.05 Town and Around; 6.30 A Whole Scene Going (teenage magazine) 7.05 United! (serial); 7.35 Get Smart! (comedy spy spoof series starring Don Adams); 8 Softly, Softly (spin-off from Z Cars, later subtitled Task Force); 8.50 News; 9.00 The Wednesday Play: Toddler on the Run ('. . .became synonymous with all that was exciting or alarming or revolutionary in television' - Halliwell); 10.15 24 Hours; 10.40 Viewpoint; 11.00 Sportsview Special; 11.50 Weather and closedown

BBC2 highlights
8.00 Call my Bluff (captained by Frank Muir and Patrick Campbell); 9.00 The Vintage Years of Hollywood

ITV Rediffusion
2.15-4.45 Racing; 4.45 Small Time; 5.00 Zoo Time (1958-65); 5.25 Adventures of Long John Silver (Australian series starring Robert Newton reprising his most memorable role); 5.55 News; 6.07 Reporting '66; 6.35 Crossroads
7.00 University Challenge ('Asking the questions, Bamber Gascoigne' since 1962); 7.30 Coronation Street; 8.00 The Fugitive starring David Janssen; 8.55 News; 9.10 Millicent (Martin); 9.40 This England (series of personal, impressionistic films); 10.25 Professional Wrestling; 11.10 News; 11.12 Shop Talk; 11.42 Dateline; 11.52 Second Generation (philosophical talking heads)

Radio highlight
Home
12.10 Down Your Way

Chart entries

5th   The Troggs, 'Wild Thing' (reached No 2)
12th   Ken Dodd, 'Promises' (No 6)
        Bob Dylan, 'Rainy Day Woman' (No 7)
        The Mamas and the Papas, 'Monday Monday'
        (No 3)
        Frank Sinatra, 'Strangers in the Night' (No 1)
        Percy Sledge, 'When a Man Loves a Woman' (No 4)
        Small Faces, 'Hey Girl' (No 10)
19th   The Rolling Stones, 'Paint it Black' (No 1)

DECLINE OF STEAM. . .

Loco sheds closed

2nd   Dumfries (67E)
22nd   Consett (52K)

Sunday 1 May
Ken Blocksidge and myself headed north to York to see the only preserved 'A3' 'Pacific', No 4472 *Flying Scotsman*, arrive with a train from London

Locomotives withdrawn

Two 'BB' 'Pacifics' were withdrawn from Salisbury, Nos 34059 *Sir Archibald Sinclair* (which spent 13 years at Woodham's Scrapyard at Barry, South Wales, before being rescued for preservation) and 34064 *Fighter Command*, and 'MN' No 35022 *Holland-America Line* from Weymouth. The last-named was bought for preservation from Barry in 1983, 17 years after its arrival there, becoming the eighth member of the class to be rescued from Barry, and leaving only two others still there. No 70000 *Britannia* herself was withdrawn from Newton Heath on the 28th, to be scheduled for preservation, and the last 'Clan' 'Pacific', No 72006 *Clan Mackenzie* was withdrawn from Carlisle Kingmoor. The last ex-GWR '5600' Class 0-6-2Ts, designed for the Welsh valleys, Nos 5605 and 6697, were withdrawn from Croes Newydd shed on the 21st (see page 53). Three IOW 0-4-4Ts, Nos W21 *Sandown*, W26 *Whitwell* and W29 *Alverstone*, were withdrawn from Ryde on the 1st.

Total steam locos withdrawn in May: 44
Cumulative total for year: 397

King's Cross, appropriately called the 'White Rose'. I photographed No 4472 standing under York station's great roof, surrounded by the usual crowd of photographers.

Sunday 1 May
We then paid a visit to York shed (51A), which is now the home of the National Railway Museum. There were several locomotives on shed, including (*top*) ex-LNER Class 'B1' 4-6-0 No 61035 (withdrawn from York on 12 December) and (*middle*) 'V2' Class 2-6-2 No 60824 (taken out of service from Edinburgh St Margaret's on 26 September).

Later in the shed yard (*bottom*), *Flying Scotsman* is being serviced before returning to London, and is seen here under the huge coaling tower. At the edge of the group of people on the right-hand side is my good friend Ken Blocksidge, who accompanied me on many journeys in 1966. Through the coaling tower can be seen several locomotives, including 'WD' 2-8-0, 'V2' 2-6-2 and a 2-6-0. Overlooking the scene is York Minster.

Tuesday 3 May
I went to Water Orton (east of Birmingham), which was the junction for the lines from Birmingham to Derby and Leicester. Although the weather was a little dull, there was quite a lot of

steam activity, and one of the first trains that I saw was a Derby-bound freight hauled by '8F' 2-8-0 No 48674. The signal box is still there today, but is used as a tool store. The well-proportioned station building can be seen above the road bridge.

Tuesday 3 May

Continuing the sequence begun by the previous picture, No 48674 is next seen taking the Derby line as a westbound coal train approaches from Leicester with another '8F' 2-8-0 in charge, this time No 48063.

The final picture shows a close-up of No 48063 as it takes the avoiding line through Water Orton station. The rear of the Derby-bound freight shows what appears to be an articulated lorry carried on two separate flat wagons. Hams Hall power station can be seen in the background of both pictures.

Saturday 7 May

By this time in 1966, the only GWR-type locomotives to be seen at work (apart from 'Castle'
Class 4-6-0 No 7029, formerly *Clun Castle*, and
preserved locomotives) were members of various
0-6-0 pannier tanks, and the sole surviving
members of the Collett Class '5600' 0-6-2Ts,
Nos 5605 and 6697, both shedded at 6C Croes
Newydd (Wrexham). This shed was originally
on the Western Region (as 89B), but had passed
to the LMR with recent boundary changes.

No 6697 is seen on the shed turntable having
finished work for the day. As we shall see shortly, the locomotive (together with No 5605) was
mainly employed shunting in the shed yard (see
pages 63-4) and occasionally on trip workings to
Brymbo, the local colliery. The 0-6-2 tank is
framed by Standard Class '4' 4-6-0 No 75010
and 0-6-0 pannier tank No 9610. The rear of an
'8F' is also visible in the yard. The two 0-6-2Ts
were withdrawn on 21 May.

'Parade of the Panniers' could be the title for this picture inside Croes
Newydd roundhouse. From left to right are Class '2F' 0-6-0PT No 1628
(the last of its class when it was withdrawn on 10 September), Class '3F'
0-6-0PT No 3704, Class '2F' No 1638 (withdrawn on 6 August) and
Class '3F' No 9610 (withdrawn on 24 September), with 4-6-0 No 75010
intruding on the right-hand side.

Sunday 8 May

The next day saw Ken and myself pay a visit to South Wales to have a look at what was slowly becoming something of a Mecca for steam enthusiasts - Barry scrapyard. The yard was owned by Dai Woodham MBE, who was to do so much for railway preservation in the UK in the following years, and was subsequently honoured by his country for that work. It is safe to say that without Dai Woodham (and of course the enthusiasts who preserved them) there would be a lot fewer locomotives running around today on main and preserved lines. On that spring day the yard was full of scrapped locomotives, and the following pictures show just a few of them (mainly those in photographable positions).

As I said in the Introduction, I sadly missed out on seeing the last rites on the Somerset & Dorset route, which had closed on 7 March; the nearest I came to it was in seeing S&D Class '7F' 2-8-0 No 53809 at Barry. This locomotive, which was designed by Fowler and introduced in 1914, was rebuilt with a larger boiler in 1925, and is now happily preserved at the Midland Railway Centre at Butterley. Over the years, it has also been a regular performer on the main line.

Another Midland Railway design of locomotive at Barry on that Sunday was represented by two Class '4F' 0-6-0s Nos 44422 and 44123. They had both been at Barry only since September 1965, and are both now preserved, having left the yard in 1977 and 1981 respectively.

There were also some ex-SR locomotives at Barry, including Class 'S15' 4-6-0 No 30506, designed by Urie in 1920 for the LSWR. It is now preserved at the Mid Hants Railway.

Naturally there were many ex-GWR locomotives at Barry, including 'King' Class 4-6-0 No 6024 *King Edward I*, which had languished at Barry since 1962, beyond it an unidentified 2-6-2T, Class '4300' 2-6-0 No 5322 (only the third loco to be rescued from Barry for preservation, in March 1969), and finally one of the powerful Class '7200' 2-8-2 tanks, No 7202.

All these GWR locomotives are now preserved. No 6024 was until recently a regular performer on the main line, and Nos 5322 and 7202 are preserved by the GW Society at Didcot.

Tuesday 10 May
Above I paid a visit to Sutton Coldfield Park, through which runs the line from Water Orton to Walsall (and to Wolverhampton and Stafford). There are still freight workings on this line today, but in 1966 many of them were steam-hauled, usually by ex-LMS '8Fs', 'Black Fives' and Standards. On that lovely spring day 2-8-0 No 48354 heads through the park in the Walsall direction with a neat-looking freight. As the locomotive has a Stoke shedplate (5D), it is reasonable to assume that it is heading for that area. It was withdrawn from its home shed on 19 November.

Left Following the previous shot, I drove back to Halesowen to see the afternoon goods to Stourbridge depart, but only just managed to get a shot of pannier tank No 9614 as it was about to bank the afternoon goods up to Old Hill.

It is worth remembering that there was no motorway link around the Birmingham area in those days, and the journey from Sutton Coldfield to Halesowen, although only about 15 miles, probably took an hour.

Friday 13 May

A few days later saw me out photographing again, this time on Bromsgrove's famous Lickey incline, near Blackwell station almost at the summit of the 1 in 37 bank. I had been told that it was doubtful that I would see any steam action, for this route (as far as Barnt Green) was now under Western Region control, on which there was a steam ban. The first picture that I took will, I am sure, be interesting to many readers 30 years on, as Type 4 'Peak' Class diesel No D113 nears the summit with a morning Bristol-Birmingham express.

Despite the date I appear to have been lucky that morning for, a few minutes later, light '8F' No 48367 headed up the bank back to the Birmingham area. I stayed around for another couple of hours, but no more steam materialised.

...

Saturday 14 May

At one time Wolverhampton was quite a railway town, what with its two busy stations, High Level (LMS) and Low Level (GWR), and its locomotive sheds, Bushbury (ex-LMS 21C), Stafford Road and Oxley (ex-GWR 84A and 84B), and the locomotive works at Stafford Road. By 1966, however, all that remained of this mini railway empire were the two stations and one locomotive shed, Oxley, now under LMR control and renumbered 2B.

While Everton were winning the Cup Final, Class '5' 4-6-0 No 45447 is seen coaling at the former GWR depot. On the left are several other 'Black Fives' and '8Fs' outside the shed.

Left and below left Inside Oxley shed were Standard Class '2MT' 2-6-0 No 78008 and Class '5700' 0-6-0PT No 3605 (both to be withdrawn during October). On the left-hand edge of both pictures is 0-6-0PT No 5770.

Sunday 15 May

Above right As I mentioned, the only ex-GWR-type tender locomotive (apart from those preserved) still working on BR was 'Castle' Class 4-6-0 No 7029, formerly *Clun Castle*, seen here being serviced at Tyseley shed, its home base. As we shall see a little later, it would sometimes work an early evening van train to and from Banbury.

Right A glance inside Tyseley's shed on that Sunday revealed 'Black Five' No 44780 and '9F' 2-10-0 No 92002 framing No 44859 and another unidentified '9F'.

Sunday 15 May

Above A quick trip round the corner, so to speak, brought me to Saltley shed, where I photographed Standard 2-6-0 No 76040, two 'Black Five' 4-6-0s and a breakdown crane.

Monday 16 May

Below A return visit to Tyseley on the following morning saw Class '2MT' 2-6-0 No 46522 pulling through Tyseley station with a long haul of loaded coal wagons, bound for the North Warwickshire line. The shed, now

renumbered 2A under LMR control, is on the left-hand side. Although Tyseley in WR days was numbered 84E - the main shed of the group being 84A Wolverhampton Stafford Road - it was the only WR shed in the Birmingham area, and thus had a large allocation of locomotives, including 'Halls' and 'Granges'.

That night I was doing a jazz gig with a good friend of mine, saxophonist and fellow railway enthusiast Mike Burney, and he told me that there was still steam at work on the Cromford & High Peak Railway in Derbyshire. We therefore decided to travel up there the following morning.

Tuesday 17 May
Mike and I duly headed for the CHPR, but we arrived too late in the day, for work had finished quite early that morning. Nevertheless I was able to get this picture of Class 'OF' 0-4-0ST No 47000 after its morning's work as it rested outside the winding house at the top of Sheep Pasture incline.

Tuesday 17 May

Without more ado, and vowing to return to the CHPR in the next few days, Mike and I headed for Westhouses shed (16G), situated on the line between Alfreton and Chesterfield, not many miles from the CHPR. In the shed yard was Class '4F' 0-6-0 No 44218, complete with tender cab (for working in the Peak District). These fine 0-6-0s were introduced by the LMS in 1924 to a Midland Railway design. Having been taken out of service on 26 March, No 44218 was awaiting scrapping; by 8 October the class was extinct (see page 149).

Another Midland design, 'Jinty' 0-6-0T No 47534 (still at work), was photographed inside the shed, surrounded by '8F' 2-8-0s and 'Peak' Class diesel No D102.

Thursday 19 May
Two days later I visited the Wrexham area again and managed to take several pictures of GWR 0-6-2T No 6697,
this time working the shed yard at Croes Newydd.

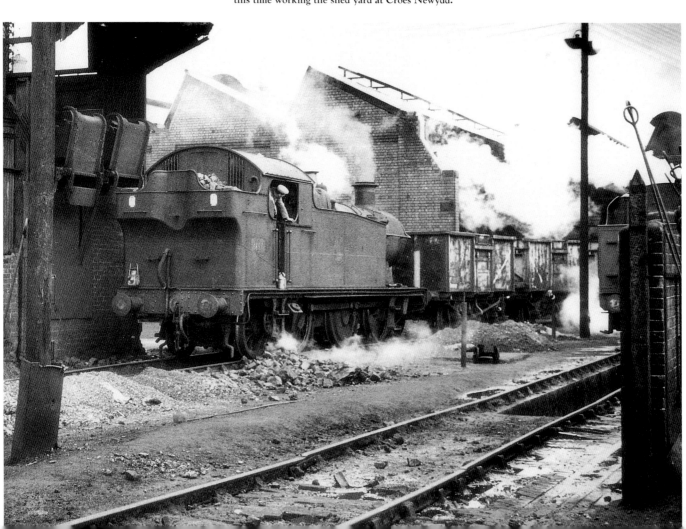

Thursday 19 May

Left A further view of No 6697 shunting in Croes Newydd shed yard. This locomotive has been preserved by the GW Society at Didcot.

Below left To complete this Great Western quartet, pannier tank No 9610 (see page 53) is seen near Broughton crossing on the same day, with a Brymbo-Wrexham coal train. Note that it still has its cabside plates.

This page From Wrexham I hurried back to Birmingham in order to see ex-LMS 'Coronation' 'Pacific' No 46235 *City of Birmingham* being towed through Snow Hill station by 'Black Five' No 45039 on their journey from Crewe Works to Saltley. From there, on the following Sunday morning (22 May), No 46235 was moved by low-loader to Birmingham Museum of Science and Industry, where it remains today.

In the first view the pair are seen in Snow Hill, then No 45039 is pictured at Duddeston Road against Saltley gas works on the evening of 19 May. The final picture shows D5180, which had assisted in the manoeuvre, No 46235, D1727 and No 45039 posing for the camera near Saltley shed (2E).

Friday 20 May
The next day I was back on the CHPR. This time No 47000 was in action and the first two pictures show the 0-4-0ST propelling a load of wagons from Sheep Pasture to the quarry at Middleton.

No 47000 pauses between shunting duties near the quarry face, then resumes its shunting duties. The locomotive was one of the early Kitson designs, being introduced in 1932. Later designs had extended side tanks and coal space. It was withdrawn less than five months later, on 8 October.

Friday 20 May

After photographing at Middleton, I carried on up the line towards Buxton. At Newhaven Farm crossing, just south of Friden, where the line crosses the A5012, I saw ex-WD 'J94' 0-6-0ST No 68006 with a load of wagons from the Buxton direction bound for Middleton Top. This section of line included the famous Hopton Incline, 1 in 14 for trains going in the Buxton direction. These useful tank locomotives had been purchased from the WD by the LNER in 1946. Nos 68006 and 68012 were to work the last trains on the CHPR when, sadly, it closed on 30 April 1967.

Saturday 21 May

The following morning I went to Water Orton again in order to photograph the 'East Midlander No 9'. This was a special train organised by the RCTS from Nottingham to Crewe Works via Walsall, Wolverhampton, Stafford, Market Drayton and Madeley, returning via Stockport, Chinley, Millers Dale and Ambergate to Nottingham. Here the special pulls through Water Orton with an immaculate Standard Class '9F' 2-10-0 in charge - the usual spotters are on the wall! Although the train is from Nottingham, it is coming in on the Leicester line, so it has probably left the Derby line at Kingsbury Junction, joining the Leicester line at Whitacre Junction, a few miles to the east of Water Orton.

Thursday 26 May

Above Mike Burney and I visited the York area, travelling overnight after a late jazz gig and thus arriving at York for an early start. Just south of York station at around 8 am we saw ex-LNER Class 'B1' 4-6-0 No 61019 (formerley *Nilghai*) heading into York with a passenger train, probably from the Doncaster area. The number of wagons and vans in the goods yard are a reminder of how much freight traffic was still carried by the railways at that time.

We must have been on this road bridge just as people were going to work, possibly at Rowntree's chocolate factory, for suddenly the road was full of what seemed to be hundreds of people on bikes.

Below We then moved on to the magnificent station, where I photographed LNER-type Class 'K1' 2-6-0 No 62028, standing by platform 8. These powerful locomotives were introduced in 1949 and were equally at home on freight as on passenger work. No 62028 did not see the year out, being

Thursday 26 May
Shortly after I took the previous picture, Standard Class '3MT' 2-6-0 No 77012 departed from one of the bay platforms on the west side of the station, with an ex-GWR signal inspection coach, bound for Darlington. No 77012, which was designed and built at Swindon in 1954, spent its working life in the North East of England, and was withdrawn in June 1967.

After York we called at Church Fenton station, which is the junction for the York-Leeds and the York-Wakefield lines. Class '9F' 2-10-0 No 92205 hurries through the neat-looking station with a southbound tank train.

Later in the day I took this photograph of very grimy Class 'B1' 4-6-0 No 61224 passing Wakefield shed with a ballast train from the Scunthorpe direction. In the last weeks of its life, it was withdrawn from Wakefield on 31 July.

The final picture of 26 May was taken at Wakefield Westgate station, and shows Class '4MT' 2-6-0 No 43125 heading through the station with a southbound goods.

Whit Sunday 29 May

Above Ken Blocksidge and I paid a visit to the London area, our first port of call being Waterloo station, where we arrived just in time to see rebuilt 'Merchant Navy' 'Pacific' No 35012 *United States Line* departing with the 'Bournemouth Belle' Pullman train.

Below After visiting Waterloo we called in at Nine Elms shed (70A), where we saw unrebuilt 'West Country' Class 'Pacific' No 34015 *Exmouth.*

Above Also outside the shed was Class 'Q1' 0-6-0 No 33006. These Bulleid Austerity-design locomotives were introduced in 1942, and an example of the class is preserved. This was one of the last three examples of the class, which had been withdrawn at the beginning of January. Behind the 0-6-0 was a Standard Class 4MT 4-6-0.

Below Inside the shed was an example of a rebuilt 'West Country' 4-6-2 No 34101 *Hartland*; withdrawn from Eastleigh in July, happily this locomotive is preserved.

Sunday 29 May

Above Our next location on this Whit Sunday was the cutting at Clapham Common, where I photographed 'West Country' 'Pacific' No 34021 *Dartmoor* rushing by in charge of the 4.30 pm Waterloo-Bournemouth train.

Below Then it was back again to Waterloo, just in time to see Class '5MT' 4-6-0 No 73155 taking water after its arrival with a train from Bournemouth. No 73155 was one of a batch built in 1956 and fitted with Caprotti valve gear.

We then returned to Clapham cutting to see the 6.30 pm Waterloo-Bournemouth hauled by rebuilt 'Battle of Britain' 4-6-2 No 34077 603 *Squadron.*

On our way home we paused at the old Transport Museum in Clapham, and through the glass doors I was able to get a picture of LNER 'Pacific' No 4468 *Mallard.* The trams also looked very interesting.

June

THE HEADLINES. . .

Wimbledon Champions are Manuel Santana of Spain and Billie Jean King of the USA.

2nd   Eamon de Valera is re-elected President of the Republic of Ireland for a further seven years, but only by 1.6%.
US spacecraft *Surveyor 1* soft-lands on the moon, as part of the planning for a manned flight to land before 1970. The US, USSR and UN talk of an International Treaty on Peaceful Uses of the Moon and other Celestial Bodies.

3-6th   Commander Cernan of *Gemini IX* makes the longest space walk ever - 2 hrs 5 mins.

20th   Curtailment of cigarette ads on press, posters and cinemas.
Coventry's PC 492, Mohamet Yusef Daar, becomes the first black policeman in Britain.

28th   The Ulster Volunteer Force is banned in Ulster.

29th   'Barclaycard', Britain's first credit card, is introduced by Barclays.

30th   Mike Tyson born, controversial US heavyweight boxer.

ENTERTAINMENT

London theatres

Whitehall: 'Come Spy With Me' with Danny La Rue, Barbara Windsor and Richard Wattis
Wyndhams: 'The Prime of Miss Jean Brodie' starring Vanessa Redgrave

Television: Thursday 2 June

BBC1
6.30 am Surveyor on the Moon - live pics; cricket all day; 4.45 Jackanory; 5.00 Blue Peter; 5.25 Tales from Europe; 5.50 Adventures of Tin Tin; 5.55 News; 6.5 Town and Around; 6.15 Cricket; 6.35 Television Top of the Form
7.00 Tomorrow's World (since 1957, presented by Raymond Baxter); 7.30 Top of the Pops (since 1964); 8.00 The Best of UNCLE; 8.50 News; 9.5 The Frost Report on . . . Food and Drink 9.30 The Pity of it All

(the first documentary on bad driving and carnage on our roads. '. . .the documentary of the year' - TV critic Philip Purser); 10.15 24 Hours; 10.50 The Making of America; 11.20 Weather and closedown

ITV Rediffusion
4.45 Small Time; 5 Junior Criss Cross Quiz; 5.25 Magic Boomerang; 5.55 News; 6.07 The Addams Family; 6.35 Crossroads
7.00 Weavers Green (twice-weekly 'soap' of rural life that lasted only six months); 7.30 Meet Mr Lucifer (1953 film starring Stanley Holloway); 8.55 News; 9.10 This Week (1956-78, in the mid-'60s regarded as TV's best current affairs programme); 9.40 The Man in Room 17 (unusual, logically solved crime story series); 10.35 News; 10.37 Peyton Place; 11.7 Royalist and Roundhead (lecture); 11.37 Dateline; 11.47 Second Generation

Radio highlight

Light
8.00 Overland Patrol (series)

Chart entries

2nd   The Animals, 'Don't Bring Me Down' (reached No 6)
The Yardbirds, 'Over Under Sideways Down' (No 10)

9th   Cilla Black, 'Don't Answer Me' (No 6)
Dave Dee, Dozy, Beaky, Mick and Tich, 'Hideaway' (No 10)
The Kinks, 'Sunny Afternoon' (No 1)
Ike & Tina Turner, 'River Deep, Mountain High' (No 3)

16th   The Beatles, 'Paperback Writer' (No 1)
23rd   Georgie Fame, 'Get Away' (No 1)
Chris Farlowe, 'Out of Time' (No 1)
The Hollies, 'Bus Stop' (No 5)
30th   Dave Berry, 'Mama' (No 5)
Los Bravos, 'Black is Black' (No 2)

DECLINE OF STEAM. . .

Lines closed

6th   Peterborough East to Market Harborough and Rugby Midland
Peterborough Nene Junction to Westwood Junction
Seaton to Luffenham

27th   Dalry (Brownhill Junction) to Elderslie via Kilbirnie
Glasgow St Enoch to Ibrox (Shields Junction)

Stations closed

6th   Peterborough East, Helpston, Ketton & Collyweston, Luffenham, Manton, Ashwell (Peterborough-Saxby, MR)
27th   Lochwinnoch (GSW)

Loco sheds closed

6th   Nuneaton (5E), Southport (8M)
13th   Closed to steam: Leicester Midland (15A) and Wellingborough (15B)

Locomotives withdrawn

The last two 'N' Class 2-6-0s, Nos 31405/408, and the last 'U' Class 2-6-0s, Nos 31639/791, were withdrawn from Guildford on the 5th (see page 80), and the last 'A1' 'Pacific' No 60145 *Saint Mungo* (see page 34) was withdrawn from York on the 19th. Other notable withdrawals were 'WC' 'Pacific' No 34038 *Lynton* on the 12th, 'BB' 'Pacific' No 34086 *219 Squadron* on the 19th, 'Jubilees' Nos 45654 *Hood* and 45660 *Rooke* on the 25th and 26th, 'A4' 'Pacific' No 60009 *Union of South Africa* on the 1st, 'A2' 'Pacific' No 60528 *Tudor Minstrel* on the 2nd, and 'Britannia' 'Pacific' No 70030 *William Wordsworth* on the 26th. Eight 'Q6' Class 0-8-0s were withdrawn, six of them from West Hartlepool, on the 5th. Standard '5MT' 4-6-0 No 73082 *Camelot*, withdrawn from Guildford on the 19th, spent 13 years at Barry before being acquired for preservation, minus a tender.

Total steam locos withdrawn in June: 71
Cumulative total for year: 468

Wednesday 1 June
It is just after 8.00 am and an unidentified Class '9F' 2-10-0 hurries towards Lapworth with an up coal train. This four-track section of the former GWR Birmingham to Paddington route is a reminder of just how busy the line from Snow Hill to the commuter belt of Solihull and district used to be.

Wednesday 1 June
Later in the day I visited Hagley station, where an unidentified 0-6-0 pannier tank is seen departing with a PW train for Stourbridge Junction. The goods yard had gone, but the 'pagoda'-roofed building on the edge of the former cattle dock is of interest.

I had a chat with the friendly signalman at Hagley who invited me into his immaculate signal box. He advised me that shortly there would be a Barry to Bescot banana train coming through, hopefully steam-hauled. A few minutes later, at about 6.00 pm, '8F' 2-8-0 No 48655 headed through the station with the freight. Just under the road bridge can be seen the beautiful GWR footbridge, which is today the subject of a preservation order.

Thursday 2 June
Above I returned to Lapworth the next morning and photographed '9F' No 92234 heading south with a short mixed goods.

Below It is strange to think that while an American spacecraft was landing on the moon, 1933-vintage pannier tank No 9774 was shunting in the yard at Halesowen in this seemingly timeless view. In the background is the Walter Somers steelworks. No 9774 was one of the last three '5700' Class 0-6-0PTs withdrawn from Tyseley on 12 November.

Wednesday 8 June
The next set of pictures were taken at Guildford. I travelled in the early hours of the morning in order to get pictures of, amongst other things, the last members of the former SR Class 'N' and 'U' 2-6-0s, both shedded at Guildford. Nos 31408 ('N' Class) and 31639 ('U' Class) are seen by the coaling stage; although they had been officially taken out of service on the 5th, both locomotives were still in steam, but were withdrawn shortly after this picture was taken.

Also seen at Guildford shed on that June morning were Class '3F' USA 0-6-0T No 30072 (*left*) and, taking water, Class '3MT' 2-6-2T No 82019 (*above right*). In the background of the second view is the main line to Portsmouth, and out of sight beyond the shed building is the appropriately named Chalk Tunnel.

The final scene at Guildford (*right*) shows Class '5MT' 4-6-0 No 73093 coming off the shed.

Wednesday 8 June
On my way back to the Midlands I stopped for a short while by the Waterloo-Basingstoke main line at Pirbright Junction, and was rewarded with this picture of 'Merchant Navy' 'Pacific' No 35013 *Blue Funnel* in charge of the 9.21 am Weymouth-Waterloo train.

Thursday 9 June
At 9.00 pm on the following evening I managed to take a picture of 'Castle' Class 4-6-0 No 7029 (formerly named *Clun Castle*) as it approached Lapworth in the fading evening light with a Banbury-Tyseley goods.

A few weeks earlier I had decided to spend a couple of weeks in Scotland, mainly on the eastern side, where there was still a lot of steam activity, with ex-LNER and pre-Grouping locomotives including 'A4' and 'A2' 'Pacifics' on the Glasgow-Aberdeen 3-hour expresses. I also applied for, and got, permits for the major sheds.

I set out on Sunday 12 June to drive the 440 miles to Aberdeen, where I planned to start my holiday. But the only motorway on the journey was from north of Wolverhampton to Carnforth, around 130 miles, the rest

of the journey being on single-carriageway A roads. I arrived at Perth, some 350 miles from home, at around 8.30 pm, so decided to call it a day and stop there overnight.

The following day (the 13th) was a disappointment, for all the Glasgow-Aberdeen trains were diesel-worked. When I arrived at Aberdeen, my visit to Ferryhill shed confirmed that the 'A4s' and 'A2s' were having routine maintenance carried out on them, but that they would be back in action on the following day.

Monday 13 June
Right One of the few pictures I took that day was of Class '5' 4-6-0 No 44998 on Ferryhill shed.

Tuesday 14 June
Below Having earlier seen Class 'A4' 'Pacific' No 60034 *Lord Faringdon* in charge of the 8.25 am Glasgow-Aberdeen service around the Niggs Bay area, but in dull weather, I went to Ferryhill shed to see it being serviced before taking out the 1.30 pm to Glasgow, 'The Grampian'. The driver is winding open the smokebox door.

Tuesday 14 June
An hour or so later, No 60034 is seen at
Aberdeen station prior to departure, then depart-
ing with the 1.30 pm to Glasgow. The locomo-
tive was withdrawn from Ferryhill on 24
August.

Above Later that afternoon I went back to Niggs Bay and photographed 'A4' No 60019 *Bittern* climbing the 1 in 94 out of Aberdeen (which can be seen in the background) with the 5.15 pm Aberdeen-Glasgow train. This locomotive lasted until 5 September, when it was withdrawn from Ferryhill, but it has been saved for preservation.

Below When I had been at Ferryhill shed earlier that day, I had been told that 'V2' Class 2-6-2 No 60813 would be working a school special back to Carnoustie that evening. So I went to Cove Bay, some 5 miles south of Aberdeen, where I photographed No 60813 climbing the 1 in 102 with the six-coach school special. No 60813 ended its active life at Dundee on 26 September.

Tuesday 14 June
My final shot of the day was taken in fading light at 9.00 pm, but shows Craiginches yard (Aberdeen) full of goods traffic as Class '5' No 44797 heads in with the 7.00 pm Perth-Aberdeen mixed passenger train.

Wednesday 15 June
I stayed overnight at Aberdeen, and the next morning, while on my way south, I spent some time on the lineside near Kinnaber Junction. As the weather was very bad, I carried on to Brechin, where, in better conditions, I was just in time to photograph former North British 0-6-0 'J37' Class No 64547 shunting in the goods shed (under the watchful eye of a youthful enthusiast) prior to returning to Montrose with the daily goods train via Bridge of Dun and Kinnaber Junction, this 3-mile section being on the Aberdeen-Perth main line. In those days the former Caledonian route from Aberdeen to Perth (and Glasgow) left the former North British line to Dundee at Kinnaber Junction, just north of Montrose. The Caledonian route was closed a few years later, so now all trains from Aberdeen to Perth and Glasgow run via Dundee. This 1914-vintage loco was withdrawn on the last day of 1966.

A short while later, another 'J37' 0-6-0, this time No 64620, crossed the Montrose basin as it headed south out of Montrose with a return afternoon goods to Dundee. Not a perfect picture, but a pleasant reminder of pre-Grouping locomotives at work.

The next picture that day was taken by the crossing keeper's house at Mildens crossing, near Coupar Angus on the main Aberdeen-Perth line. The locomotive is 'A4' No 60019 *Bittern* again, with the 5.15 pm Aberdeen-Glasgow train.

Wednesday 15 June
I arrived at Perth station at 9.00 pm that evening, where I saw 'V2' No 60813 again waiting in the middle road by the Dundee platforms.

An hour or so later the rain set in. No 60813 is now waiting, at just after 10.00 pm, to leave Perth with the 10.30 pm to Dundee. This is a hand-held shot at ¼ second at f1.8. I had by then decided to base myself at Perth for the next week or so, and I stayed at a very pleasant hotel near the station, which specialised in traditional Scottish high teas.

Thursday 16 June
The first shot next morning was of *Bittern* once again, having just arrived at Perth station with the 8.25 am Glasgow-Aberdeen train. The man running along the platform is perhaps a passenger who is taking advantage of the stop to get a photograph of the train before it leaves. The fireman and the guard are looking a little anxious, wondering if he is going to make it! Note the ornate station lamp.

Thursday 16 June
Next I went to Thornton Junction in the Kingdom of Fife, where my visit to the shed (62A) revealed Class 'B1' 4-6-0 No 61344 simmering away inside the building. Just outside the shed is a 'WD' 2-8-0.

On leaving the shed I went to photograph on the Dunfermline-Thornton line near Cluny, a couple of miles east of Thornton Junction, in the hope of seeing a Gresley Class 'J38' 0-6-0 at work. I was not to be disappointed, for within a short while of arriving at this location, I was able to photograph No 65914 of that class, heading for Thornton with a train of scrap metal and coal. The locomotive was withdrawn in November.

JUNE

At the same location, but heading in the Dunfermline direction, I photographed a coal train hauled by Class 'WD' 2-8-0 No 90596.

On leaving Thornton, I travelled to Stanley Junction, some 7 miles north of Perth, where I got my first view of ex-LNER 'A2' 'Pacific' No 60532 *Blue Peter* as it headed for Perth with the 1.30 pm Aberdeen-Glasgow train, 'The Grampian'. The Highland line to Inverness can be seen coming in from the left behind a very modern-looking signal box. *Blue Peter* was the last 'A2' in service, and was withdrawn on New Year's Eve 1966; it is now preserved.

After taking a few more pictures around Perth station in dull light, I called it a day.

Friday 17 June
This page The next morning the light was good, and I was at Perth station to see No 60019 once more; it arrived and took water, then departed for Aberdeen with the 8.25 am from Glasgow.

Above right After seeing *Bittern* depart from Perth, I drove over to Dundee, where in the busy goods yard was Class 'J37' 0-6-0 No 64602, acting as yard pilot.

Right I called in at Dundee shed before leaving the area and was able to photograph 'V2' 2-6-2 No 60919 on the shed turntable. Two and a half months later, on 2 September, the locomotive was taken out of service from this shed.

Friday 17 June

Above After leaving Dundee I decided to travel back to Perth to see the 1.30 pm Aberdeen-Glasgow, hopefully again hauled by No 60532. Although by this time the weather had gone dull, I was rewarded by the sight of *Blue Peter* heading out of Perth with the southbound 'Grampian'.

Below A little later that Friday afternoon I was in luck once again, this time in seeing 'Britannia' 'Pacific' No 70038 (formerly *Robin Hood*) heading out of Perth with the 8.00 am Birmingham-Aberdeen service. Apart from one light engine working, this was the only time I saw a 'Britannia' working on the eastern side of Scotland.

My final picture of the day was of Standard Class '4MT' 2-6-4T No 80028 prior to departure from Perth with the 7.00 pm to Aberdeen. From the exposed areas of the platforms it can be seen that by now it was raining quite heavily. No 80028 was a 26 September withdrawal from Perth.

Saturday 18 June

The following day was much brighter. The first picture I took was of a group of young train-spotters watching Class 'B1' 4-6-0 No 61263 with an empty stock train at the southern end of Perth station, which at that time still had an entrance from the long road bridge that spans it. This locomotive was another New Year's Eve 1966 casualty.

Saturday 18 June

After taking a couple more pictures around Perth, I went over to Greenhill Junction, where the line from Perth to Glasgow meets the two routes from Edinburgh to Glasgow that diverge at Polmont Junction, east of Falkirk. On this sunny Saturday afternoon ex-WD 2-8-0 No 90071 climbs through the station and heads for the Fife coalfields with a train of empties from the Glasgow area, to be followed later by Class 'B1' 4-6-0 No 61140 (with self-weighing tender) in charge of a Leven-Garelochhead troop train. Like the 'B1' seen on the previous page, No 61140 was withdrawn on 31 December.

Opposite page I finished up at Perth shed that evening, where Class '5' 4-6-0 No 44720 was basking in the late evening sun. Seen also in the first view is No 44696. No 44720 ended its working life on 27 October.

Sunday 19 June

Above left I decided to visit Edinburgh via the newly opened (1964) Forth Road Bridge to have a look at St Margaret's shed, and also photograph the Carstairs-Edinburgh trains, which were still steam-hauled but now terminated at Waverley station, Princes Street having closed the previous year.

Outside St Margaret's shed that Sunday lunchtime was Class '5' 4-6-0 No 45053, and inside the shed can be seen a row of 2-6-4 tank engines, headed by No 80055; just behind No 45053 is 'V2' No 60919. St Margaret's shed had an allocation of around 200 locomotives in its heyday, when it was the principal shed for the Waverley route, but by now there were only about a dozen shedded there. It was closed to steam later in the year, and none of the identified locomotives saw 1967.

Left After a browse round the shed I went to Waverley station, where Class '5' 4-6-0 No 45469 had just arrived with the 2.35 pm from Carstairs.

This page I then went up to Princes Street Gardens where, after a long wait, I photographed No 45168 in charge of the 6.40 pm from Carstairs. The 'going-away' shot shows the train about to enter The Mound Tunnel. Through the tunnel portal on the left can be glimpsed one of Waverley station's many platforms.

While I was at this location, I met fellow photographers Graham Mallinson and Tim Stephens, who were to team up with me during the following week's photographic 'bash'.

Monday 20 June

The second week of my Scottish trip started well enough, with Class '5' No 44794 pulling out of Perth with the 9.50 am to Aberdeen in bright sunshine. Earlier I had attempted to photograph No 60019 again with the 8.25 am Glasgow-Aberdeen in Hilton cutting. This had not been very successful, but later in the week (see page 104) I managed to get a better picture with 60019 at the same location.

After photographing at Perth, we went over to Dunfermline shed to see North British (LNER Class 'J36') 0-6-0 No 65288. This modern-looking shed contrasts sharply with this handsome veteran locomotive, which was introduced in 1888.

JUNE

On our way back to Perth we stopped near the northern portal of Hilton Tunnel, just in time to see 'B1' Class 4-6-0 No 61349 heading downhill into Perth with a mixed goods from Bridge of Earn, which is just over a mile from Hilton Junction on the Ladybank route through Fife to Edinburgh.

Tuesday 21 June
The first picture that I took was of Class 'V2' 2-6-2 No 60813 again, crossing the River Tay at Perth with the 8.20 am ECS working from Dundee.

Tuesday 21 June

Above The previous photograph was followed shortly by a panned shot of *Bittern* at speed near Luncarty (just north of Perth) with the 8.25 am Glasgow-Aberdeen train.

Left The next shot shows 'J38' 0-6-0 No 65914 (see also page 90) climbing out of Thornton Junction (working wrong line) with a heavy freight train bound for Dunfermline. The location is near Cluny.

Above right Although the last picture was taken in sunshine, by the time we arrived at our next location, which was Forgandenny, just south of Perth (in order to see the 1.30 pm Aberdeen-Glasgow train) it had started to rain, and when 'A2' No 60532 *Blue Peter* appeared with the Glasgow train, the heavens had really opened with a thunderstorm.

Wednesday 22 June

Right The following day the weather was slightly better, and the first shot was of No 60813 once again, only this time a back shot of the 8.20 am ECS from Dundee as it headed across the River Tay into Perth. This view clearly shows the two distinct styles of bridges, with the two modern metal bridges contrasting with the older brick bridge built by Telford.

'A4' 'Pacific' No 60019 *Bittern* heads through Hilton Junction with the 8.25 am Glasgow-Aberdeen train. The line on the left is to Edinburgh via Ladybank. This also led to the Glenfarg route to Edinburgh, which left the Ladybank route just east of Bridge of Earn. The Glenfarg route closed in 1965. Hilton Junction signal box can be seen just beyond the signal gantry.

We next moved on to Dundee, and by now the weather was beginning to improve. Posing on Dundee shed (62B) is ex-LNER Class 'A2' 4-6-2 No 60530 *Sayajirao* alongside my old friend 'V2' Class 2-6-2 No 60813. The complicated telegraph pole is worthy of note! *Sayajirao* was withdrawn from Dundee on 19 November.

One of the reasons that we had gone over to Dundee was to see the 1.30 pm Dundee to Montrose goods, usually worked by a Class 'J37' 0-6-0 (ex-NBR). The first photograph shows No 64602 (see also page 93) being serviced at Dundee shed, prior to taking out the Montrose goods. On the left is Class '2MT' 2-6-0 No 46464; withdrawn from Dundee on 17 August, it is now preserved on the Strathspey Railway, Aviemore.

The second shot, taken near Broughty Ferry, some 5 miles east of Dundee, shows the North British 0-6-0 'going like a good 'un' as it heads for Montrose.

Wednesday 22 June

We decided to leave Perth and travel to Hawick in order that on the following day we would be able to see the Thursdays-only 10.25 am Morpeth to Woodburn train. On our way we stopped just south of Gleneagles to see No 60532 once again with the 1.30 pm Aberdeen-Glasgow train.

Thursday 23 June

The next morning, as is quite often the case when you go after a rare working, the weather was truly awful, as can be seen from these two pictures of ex-NER 0-6-0 (Class 'J27') No 65814, as it enters Scots Gap station with the 10.25 am from Morpeth to Woodburn, and takes water there. This locomotive was in the last week of its active life, being withdrawn from Blyth on the 29th.

This line originally ran to Reedsmouth, which was the junction for Hexham to the south and Riccarton Junction (on the Waverley Route) to the north-west.

Friday 24 June
After our wet interlude in the Border country, we travelled across to Ayr in the south-west of Scotland, hoping to see the ex-LMS 'Crab' 2-6-0s at work. After staying the night in Ayr, we called in at the shed on the Friday morning only to be told that there no 'Crabs' at work that day, so the only shot I got of one was of No 42737 outside the shed. It was withdrawn on 29 November.

However, other steam was at work in the area, and we went to Annbank Junction, east of Ayr, where the line from Drongan and Killoch meets the line from Mauchline Junction. The first picture shows Class '5' No 45167 taking the line to Drongan with coal empties, while sister locomotive No 44989 waits to come off the line from Mauchline Junction with a freight for Ayr.

Some time later, No 45167 is seen in the second view approaching Annbank Junction with a load of coal from the Drongan area.

Friday 24 June

After our visit to Ayr we travelled to Carlisle, where I was to drop Graham and Tim, who were going on to the Waverley Route for a special, but on the way we called first at Beattock summit, where Class '5' No 45259 is seen heading north with a parcels train.

We then stopped on the road bridge just north of Beattock station, where Class '4MT' 2-6-4 tank No 42058 (which would be withdrawn on 24 August) was giving a helping hand to a north-bound goods. The small goods yard and locomotive shed can be seen clearly.

Having said goodbye to my travelling companions for the last week (whom incidentally I still meet on the lineside from time to time today), I made my way south to Penrith, where I stayed overnight in readiness to photograph around Tebay and Shap the following day.

Saturday 25 June

The following morning started fine, but it was not to last. I managed to get a picture of 'Britannia' 'Pacific' No 70009 (formerly *Alfred the Great*) heading north over Dillicar troughs, followed by Class '5' No 45094 with a northbound goods train before the bad weather set in. After taking a few more pictures around Scout Green in indifferent light, I decided to call it a day and head for home after my two-week 'bash'. On reflection, probably I

should have gone over to the Waverley Route with Graham and Tim, but we all make mistakes. . .

Between the end of my Scottish trip and the end of June I took several pictures of the coal trains on the Severn Valley line between Bewdley and Highley, most of which were published last year in my 'British Railways Past & Present Special' volume on the Severn Valley Railway.

July

THE HEADLINES. . .

6-8th PM Harold Wilson meets French PM Pompidou to approve the Channel Tunnel project.

11th The merger of BMC and Jaguar Cars is announced.

14th Harold Wilson announces economic emergency measures - a freeze on incomes, prices and dividends, including Surtax, Post Office charges up, Purchase Tax up.

17th 19-year-old Jim Ryan from the USA sets a new record for running the mile, 3 mins 51.3 secs.

18th Exploratory talks are held with Argentina concerning the Falkland Islands.

18-21st The successful docking and space walk from *Gemini X* represent the most successful and complicated space mission so far.

21st Gwynfor Evans becomes the first Welsh Nationalist MP.

28th Florence Nagle takes the Jockey Club to court for not allowing women to have licences to train racehorses.

29th Bob Dylan crashes his motorcycle and does not perform for a year.

30th In the World Cup Final at Wembley, England win 4-2 in extra time. For scoring a hat-trick Geoff Hurst is entitled to take the ball, but a German player, Helmut Haller, takes it. He confesses in April 1996 and agrees to return it.

ENTERTAINMENT

Entrances and exits

13th Bridget Bardot marries Gunther Sachs
23rd Montgomery Clift dies from a heart attack, aged 45

London theatres

Royal Festival Hall: Georgian State Dance Company of the USSR
Fortune: 'The Bellow Plays' with Miriam Karlin and Harry Towb

Television: Sunday 24th July

BBC1
1.30 Gardening Club; 1.50 Farming; 2.20 Motor Racing; 2.45 World Cup Match of the Week; 3.35 Film Show Business; 5.05 The Loner (Western series with Lloyd Bridges); 5.30 Dutch Grand Prix; 6.10 News; 6.15 Meeting Point; 6.45 Story; 6.50 Songs of Praise; 7.25 Perry Mason; 8.15 The Ken Dodd Show; 9.00 Thirteen Against Fate; 10.00 News; 10.10 Burning Issue: Sex and Violence in Art; 11.00 Meeting Point; 11.30 Weather and closedown

BBC2 highlights
Cricket, and at 10.10 An Enemy of the State (six-part serial)

ATV
2.50 Police Five, with Shaw Taylor; 3.00 World Cup Report; 3.35 Man of the World, starring Craig Stevens; 4.35 Danger Man (spy series providing a pre-*Prisoner* role for Patrick McGoohan; 5.30 The Forest Rangers (Canadian children's adventure series); 6.00 News; 6.15 Tinga and Tucker with Jean Morton; 6.35 The Singing People; 6.55 In View; 7.25 The Rifleman (Western series starring Chuck Connors); 7.55 Alexander the Great (film with Richard Burton, Frederic March and Claire Bloom); 9.55 News; 10.05 Blackpool Show; 11.05 The Human Jungle (drama series starring psychiatrist Herbert Lom); 12.00 Asking For It

Radio highlights

Light
12.00 Family Favourites; 1.30 The Morecambe & Wise Show; 2.00 The Mitchell Minstrels; 2.30 Frankie Howerd; 3.00 Melody Hour; 4.00 Pick of the Pops

Chart entries

7th David & Jonathan, 'Lovers of the World Unite, (reached No 7)
Elvis Presley, 'Love Letters' (No 6)
Dusty Springfield, 'Going Back' (No 10)
14th The Lovin' Spoonful, 'Summer in the City' (No 8)
The Troggs, 'With a Girl Like You' (No 1)
21st Cliff Richard, 'Vision' (No 7)
28th The Beach Boys, 'God Only Knows' (No 2)

DECLINE OF STEAM. . .

Line closed

4th   Ardsley to Laisterdyke via Morley Top

Stations closed

4th   Armley Moor, Bramley, Laisterdyke (Leeds-Bradford, GN); Berry Brow (L&Y); Scarborough Londesborough Road (NER)

Loco shed closed

11th   Stourbridge Junction (2C)

Locomotives withdrawn

Named locos withdrawn during the month were 'WC' 'Pacific' No 34101 *Hartland*

Sunday 3 July
I paid a visit to Stourbridge shed, which still had a reasonable number of locomotives allocated to it, including '8Fs', 'Black Fives' and ex-GWR pannier tanks.

The first picture shows '8Fs' Nos 48550, 48559, 48655 and 48610, plus two unidentified members of that class of the left-hand side.

In the second picture are 0-6-0 pannier tanks Nos 3607 (withdrawn in October) and 9608. Other panniers on shed that day were Nos 3619, 4646, 4696, 8718, 8767, 9614 and 9641. Nos 9608 and 9614 were withdrawn within three weeks, and most of the rest did not survive the year.

(acquired from Barry in April 1978 for preservation - see page 73), 'MN' 'Pacific' No 35017 *Belgian Marine*, 'Jubilee' No 45596 *Bahamas* (also now preserved), and 'A4' 'Pacific' No 60004 *William Whitelaw*. Seven '5700' Class 0-6-0PTs were withdrawn, together with 11 'Black Fives' (the majority from Scotland), ten '8Fs', six 'B1s' and five '9Fs'. Amongst the oldest locos withdrawn was 'J36' 0-6-0 No 65243 *Maude*, of 1888 vintage. By contrast, Standard '4MT' 4-6-0 No 75078, built in January 1956 and withdrawn from Eastleigh on the 10th, was rescued from Barry in June 1972, and when restored in 1977 ran on the Keighley & Worth Valley Railway, where it starred in the 1978 film *Yanks*.

Total steam locos withdrawn in July: 83
Cumulative total for year: 551

Thursday 7 July

Above I went up the Severn Valley line and photographed '8F' 2-8-0 No 48460 between Arley and Northwood Halt with a coal train from Highley, probably bound for Stourport power station.

Perhaps not the best of pictures, but I was caught by surprise, as you can see, in a very awkward location by the side of the river. By this time, part of the SVR was in the throes of preservation, and has gone on to be one of the finest preserved lines in the country.

Saturday 9 July

Left Ken Blocksidge and I were out photographing on the Cambrian line between Shrewsbury and Welshpool. Here we see BR Standard Class '4MT' 2-6-0 No 76038 heading westwards near Yockleton with the down 'Cambrian Coast Express'.

Monday 11 July

Above right On the Sunday I decided to spend a few days in the North of England, so travelled up to Skipton that evening, staying there overnight in order to get an early start on the Monday morning.

I decided to photograph between Skipton and Hellifield, but as it was Monday, goods traffic was sparse. However, around lunchtime I managed to photograph Standard Class '4MT' 4-6-0 No 75058 as it headed south out of Hellifield in the Skipton direction with a train mainly composed of tanks.

Right Some time later that day I caught No 75058 again as it entered Gargrave station with a northbound freight.

Monday 11 July
Above In the evening I spent some time at Skipton station, where ex-LMS Class '2MT' 2-6-2 tank No 41241 was seen shunting a van at the southern end of the station. The time was 8.45 pm. Following withdrawal on 10 December, this locomotive was subsequently preserved on the Keighley & Worth Valley Railway.

Tuesday 12 July
Below The following day I finished up at Leeds City station, where ex-LMS 'Jubilee' Class 4-6-0 No 45675 (formerly *Hardy*) was waiting to leave with the 8.43 pm to Sheffield.

Wednesday 13 July

I stayed overnight at Wakefield, and the next day, before heading back to the Midlands, I was out on the Goole line near Wakefield in order to photograph the ex-WD 2-8-0s that worked in the area. In the first picture No 90123 heads for Wakefield with a coal train, probably from the Featherstone area. The second scene shows sister engine No 90430 heading out of Wakefield with coal empties.

Friday 15 July

Left Back home I photographed Class '5' 4-6-0 No 44762 near Lyde Green with a goods from the Birmingham area to Stourbridge Junction. The locomotive was withdrawn on 26 November.

Monday 18 July

Below left I visited the Harbury area, north of Banbury, where 'Black Five' No 44865 was photographed heading south out of Harbury Tunnel with a heavy mineral train.

Wednesday 20 July

Right I travelled to Lymington, on the edge of the New Forest, in order to photograph Southern steam on the main line, as well as the Lymington and Swanage branches and, if possible, to have a day trip to the Isle of Wight, where the ex-LSWR 0-4-4 tank locomotives (Class 'O2') still worked the trains on the only remaining line, between Ryde and Shanklin. I arrived in the late afternoon, and one of the first shots I took was of Standard Class '4MT' 2-6-4T No 80019 nearing Brockenhurst (but still on the Lymington branch) with the 6.18 pm from Lymington; the branch joined the main Bournemouth line just south of Brockenhurst.

Below On the main Waterloo-Bournemouth line near Brockenhurst, 'Merchant Navy' 'Pacific' No 35030 *Elder Dempster Lines* heads for Bournemouth with a train from Waterloo.

Wednesday 20 July
Above To finish the day I photographed 2-6-2T No 41316 crossing the river at Lymington with an evening working from Brockenhurst. The locomotive was withdrawn from Bournemouth on 2 October.

Thursday 21 July
Below The following morning I decided to travel to the Isle of Wight and took the train from Lymington Town station to Lymington Pier, where I boarded the ferry for the short crossing to Yarmouth. This view was taken from the train (hauled by No 80019) on the approach to Lymington Pier.

Above Since Yarmouth lay some 15 miles from Ryde, I had originally planned to take my car to the island, but the ferry was so busy - you had to book in advance - that I could not. So when I arrived at Yarmouth I took a taxi (hang the expense!) across to Ryde via St John's, just south of the town, where I took my first picture, of 0-4-4T No 31 *Chale* with the 10.55 am Shanklin to Ryde.

Below A short while afterwards, on the double-track section near St John's, No 35 *Freshwater*, complete with vintage stock, climbs out of the station with the 11.19 am Ryde to Shanklin. This locomotive was to be withdrawn in October.

Thursday 21 July

Top On arriving at Ryde, and having paid off the taxi driver, the first shot I took was of No 31 again, leaving the Esplanade station with the 12.10 pm to Shanklin. The station can be seen on the left-hand side, and below me is the entrance to Ryde Tunnel, which the train is about to enter. To complete the picture is a fine array of what would now be vintage coaches, all part of the seaside scene.

Middle No 33 *Bembridge* leaves Ryde Esplanade station for the terminus of the line at Ryde Pierhead. The train is a midday working from Shanklin.

Bottom I decided to travel to Brading, midway between Ryde and Shanklin, and what better way to do so than by the train - namely the 1.10 pm from Ryde, hauled by No 24 *Calbourne*, seen here about to enter Ryde Tunnel.

Above right On arrival at Brading, which had been the junction for the Bembridge branch, closed in 1953, I first of all photographed No 24 as it pulled out of the station past the SR rail-built signal, with the 1.10 pm from Ryde. These vintage locomotives were first introduced in 1889, and fitted with Westinghouse brakes for the Isle of Wight service in 1923. Their bunkers also were enlarged, in 1932. It is nice to know that No 24 is preserved at Havenstreet on the Isle of Wight Steam Railway.

Right The next shot shows No 16 *Ventnor* just north of Brading, with the 3.19 pm Shanklin to Ryde train.

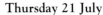
Thursday 21 July

Top and middle At Brading I took the 3.55 pm train from Shanklin back to Ryde (hauled once again by No 24), and when I arrived at Ryde Esplanade station, before I caught the bus to Yarmouth for the ferry to Lymington, I photographed No 16 as it arrived with the 4.25 pm to Shanklin, and also the tram that ran from the town to the pier alongside the BR line. The pier buildings and the funnel of an Isle of Wight ferry can be seen on the left-hand side.

Bottom After arriving at Lymington, I took the 7.15 pm to Brockenhurst (hauled by No 41316) and alighted at Lymington Town station, after a very enjoyable day at the seaside.

Right As it was still sunny, I decided to finish off the day on the main line near Brockenhurst, and some time around 8.00 pm I took this picture of 'Merchant Navy' No 35030 *Elder Dempster Lines* heading for Bournemouth with a train from Waterloo. The edge of the New Forest dominates the background. Just above the locomotive on the right-hand side can be seen the Lymington branch.

Friday 22 July

Right I started off the next day with a photograph of No 80019 again near Lymington with the 8.10 am Lymington-Brockenhurst train.

Friday 22 July

Above After that I drove over to Corfe, where from the castle grounds I photographed 2-6-4T No 80138 approaching Corfe station with the 1.25 pm Wareham to Swanage train. This locomotive was taken out of service from Bournemouth on 2 October.

Below A little later in the afternoon, Class '2MT' 2-6-2T No 41230 crossed Corfe Common with the 2.10 pm Wareham-Swanage train. Happily, part of this former Southern Railway branch line has been preserved following its closure in January 1972.

Above Back in the Brockenhurst area early that evening, I photographed 'Merchant Navy' 4-6-2 No 35012 *United States Line* as it skirted the edge of the New Forest with a down express.

These powerful 'Pacifics' were first introduced in 1941, complete with 'air-smoothed' casings like the original 'West Country' and 'Battle of Britain' 'Pacifics', but they were all rebuilt around 1956, with Walschaerts valve gear and modified details.

Saturday 23 July

Below I headed back to the Midlands the next day, but before leaving the Southern Region I was able to take a few pictures, including this one of 'West Country' 'Pacific' No 34095 *Brentor* near Beaulieu Road, with an up mid-morning express. Unlike the 'Merchant Navy' Class, only some of the 'West Country' and 'Battle of Britain' 'Pacifics' were modified. The rebuilding included the fitting of Walschaerts valve gear, and took place around 1957.

Tuesday 26 July
Above left I was busy with music for the next few days, so I was unable to travel far. I therefore spent some time at Hatton bank, where I photographed ex-LMS Class '8F' 2-8-0 No 48477 working hard on the bank with a heavy and neat-looking goods train bound for the Birmingham area.

Saturday 30 July
Left I was out photographing on the Preston-Blackpool line around Salwick, where there were also water troughs to the east of Salwick station between there and Lea. Most people will remember this day as England won the football World Cup, but having forgotten to bring my portable radio with me, it was only around 6.00 pm that day that I found out (to my immense pleasure) that we had beaten Germany.

One of the first pictures I took that day was of 'Britannia' 'Pacific' No 70006 (formerly *Robert Burns*) with a mid-morning up passenger train.

Above The 'Britannia' was followed quickly by 'Black Five' No 44915 heading a Blackpool-Glasgow train.

Right I had also come to the Blackpool line with the hope of seeing a 'Jubilee' locomotive at work, possibly from Leeds or Bradford, and I was not to be disappointed, as No 45565 *Victoria* approached Salwick station with a Blackpool-Bradford train.

August

THE HEADLINES. . .

5th John Lennon makes his much misinterpreted and misquoted claim on US Radio that the Beatles are more popular than Christ.

6th The Ministry of Social Security is created.

10th The US launches the first moon satellite, *Orbiter 1*.

18th The Queen opens the Tay Road Bridge.

27th Francis Chichester sets off from Plymouth on his round-the-world voyage.

29th The Beatles play their last live concert at Candlestick Park, San Francisco.

ENTERTAINMENT

Exits

3rd Lenny Bruce dies from a drugs overdose, aged 40.
23rd Francis X. Bushman dies, aged 83. A star of the silent era, and once known as the handsomest man in the world, he was in the original 1926 *Ben Hur* and played bit parts into the 1960s.

Television: Tuesday 16 August

BBC1
4.45 Jackanory; 5.00 The Stranger; 5.25 A Way to Adventure; 5.50 The Adventures of Tin Tin; 6.05 Town and Around; 6.30 Travellers' Tales; 6.55 Points of View, with Robert Robinson
7.00 The Newcomers; 7.30 Steptoe & Son (1964-73); 8.00 The Love Affair: The Great Man's Lady (1941 film starring Barbara Stanwyck); 8.50 News; 9.05 Film Part 2; 9.45 War against Crime; 10.15 24 Hours; 10.50 The Painter and His World; 11.20 Weather and closedown

BBC2 highlights
7.30 Home Cooking; 8.00 International Cabaret

ITV Rediffusion
2.15 Racing; 4.45 Small Time; 5.00 Five O'Clock Club; 5.25 Orlando; 5.55 News; 6.07 Batman; 6.35 Crossroads 7.00 All About You; 7.30 Emergency-Ward 10;
8.00 Love Story (drama anthology series); 8.55 News; 9.10 The FBI (crime series starring Efrem Zimbalist Jnr); 10.05 This England; 10.35 News; 10.37 Peyton Place; 11.07 Shop Talk; 11.37 Dateline; 11.47 Faith and the Word

Radio highlight

Light
10.00 Russ Conway

Chart entries

4th Manfred Mann, 'Just Like a Woman' (reached No 10)
Napoleon XIV, 'They're Coming to Take Me Away Ha Ha' (No 4)
11th The Beatles, 'Yellow Submarine/Eleanor Rigby' (No 1)
Cliff Bennett & the Rebel Rousers, 'Got to Get You Into My Life' (No 6)
Lee Dorsey, 'Working in The Coalmine' (No 8)
The Small Faces, 'All Or Nothing' (No 1)
18th Roy Orbison, 'Too Soon To Know' (No 3)
Jim Reeves, 'Distant Drums' (No 1)

DECLINE OF STEAM. . .

Loco sheds closed

1st Aviemore (formerly 60B)
29th Bathgate (64F)

Locomotives withdrawn

'Jubilee' No 45581 *Bihar & Orissa* was withdrawn from Farnley on the 7th (see page 37), 'A4' 'Pacific' No 60034 *Lord Faringdon* from Aberdeen Ferryhill on the 24th (see pages 83-4), and 'Britannia' 'Pacific' No 70050 Firth of Clyde from Carlisle Kingmoor on the 6th. Fifteen 'Black Fives' were withdrawn during the month, as well as five Ivatt '2MT' 4-6-0s, 15 '8Fs', and 28 BR Standard locos of various classes, including six 2-6-0s of the 76000 series and 10 2-6-4Ts of the 80000 series, none more than 15 years old.

Total steam locos withdrawn in August: 88
Cumulative total for year: 639

Tuesday 2 August

August was a busy month for me musically, so I was only able to manage day trips. On 2 August I photographed the Shrewsbury-Chester trains, which were still steam-hauled by Class 5 4-6-0s. The first picture, taken at Haughton, south of Gobowen, shows 4-6-0 No 45231 speeding south with a midday Chester-Shrewsbury train. The flagman casts a critical eye at the locomotive, obviously not expecting anything northbound! This of course was before 'visivests'.

In the second scene we see sister locomotive No 44863 climbing up from Chirk viaduct with an afternoon Chester-Shrewsbury train.

Thursday 4 August

My second 'day trip' was to the Duffield area, a few miles north of Derby. For most of the day the weather was awful, and it was only round tea-time, when it finally stopped raining, that I was able to take any pictures, including this one of '8F' No 48117 on the Midland main line just south of Duffield with an up freight.

A short while later I photographed another '8F' 2-8-0, this time No 48662 as it burst out of Millfield Tunnel (just north of Duffield) with northbound coal empties.

Saturday 6 August

Opposite page I was out again on the Cambrian route around the Welshpool area, first of all at Plas-y-Court, where Standard Class '4MT' 4-6-0 No 75002 heads towards Shrewsbury with the 11.45 am from Pwllheli.

The second picture shows a short goods train at Trewern, some 4 miles east of Welshpool, hauled by Class '5' 4-6-0 No 45430. During my visits to the Cambrian this is the only time that I saw a 'Black Five' on the line. This particular locomotive had barely two months of active life left, being withdrawn from Shrewsbury on 1 October.

Thursday 11 August

A wet scene on Old Hill bank as ex-GWR pannier tank 0-6-0 No 4646 (banked by another pannier tank) climbs the bank with an evening Halesowen to Langley goods. Nos 4646, 4696 (see page 111) and 9774 (page 79) were the last three surviving '5700' Class 0-6-0PTs when withdrawn on 12 November.

Saturday 13 August

With the closure of the Great Central line as a through route between Aylesbury and Rugby scheduled for 3 September, various special trains were run on the route. This one, the 'Great Central' tour, was run by the RCTS, and a variety of locomotives were used. Here we see unrebuilt 'West Country' 'Pacific' No 34002 *Salisbury*, complete with SR stock (the special started from Waterloo), about to enter Catesby Tunnel, just north of Charwelton, on the outward section of the tour.

Saturday 20 August

It was a beautiful summer's day and fortunately I spent it on the Cambrian line around Talerddig bank, between Machynlleth to the west and Newtown to the east, a lovely part of mid-Wales. It was also a good day for fans of English cricket, as the English tail-enders John Snow and Ken Higgs shared a last-wicket partnership of 128 against the West Indies, a record for England at home. This time I had remembered to bring my portable radio,

so as well as photographing steam trains in good sunshine, I was able to keep up with the Test Match.

One of the first trains I photographed that day was the up 'Cambrian Coast Express', hauled by Standard Class '4MT' 2-6-0 No 76038 and '4MT' 4-6-0 No 75010. The location is near the summit of Talerddig bank. Thirteen-year-old No 76038 was within a few weeks of withdrawal, being taken out of service from Machynlleth on 10 September.

Saturday 20 August

Above left The next shot I took was of 4-6-0s Nos 75012 and 75016 as they head down the bank with the 8.05 am Birmingham-Pwllheli train.

Left A mile or so further down the bank I took this picture of 4-6-0 No 75004 with the 8.20 am down Paddington.

Above Not long afterwards 4-6-0s Nos 75012 and 75020 were photographed climbing up Talerddig with the 10.55 am Pwllheli to Birmingham train. No 75012, which was seen on an earlier train to Pwllheli, had no doubt come off at Machynlleth, hence its rapid return.

Saturday 27 August

Next weekend I went to Talerddig again, but the weather was not so good, and I had to leave early for a 'gig' that night. However, 4-6-0s Nos 75022 and 75010 made a stirring sight with the up 'Cambrian' as they approached the summit of the bank.

September

THE HEADLINES. . .

3rd   Capt John Ridgeway and Sgt Chay Blyth reach Inishmore after rowing across the Atlantic in 91 days.

8th   The Severn Bridge is opened by the Queen, the seventh longest bridge in the world. Thirty years later, in May 1996, a second crossing will be opened.

16th   HMS *Resolution*, Britain's first Polaris submarine, is launched by the Queen Mother at Vickers in Barrow.

ENTERTAINMENT

At the cinema

Films released during the last four months of the year included *The Sand Pebbles* starring Steve McQueen (nominated for five Oscars); *Torn Curtain* starring Paul Newman and Julie Andrews, Alfred Hitchcock's 50th film; *A Man for All Seasons* starring Paul Scofield, Robert Shaw, etc, and winner of Five Oscars, including best Picture; and *The Bible*, directed by John Huston in 'Dimension 150' (70 mm) - 'At a time when religion needs all the help it can get, John Huston may have set its cause back a couple of thousand years' (Rex Reed).

London theatres

Royal Albert Hall: The Henry Wood Promenade Concerts
Comedy: 'Let's Get a Divorce' starring Fenella Fielding
Duke of York's: 'Public and Confidential', with John Gregson and Constance Cummings

Television: Wednesday 14th September

BBC1
4.45 Jackanory; 5.00 Hector Heathcote (Terrytoons cartoon); 5.25 Look at the Birds of Teesmouth; 5.50 The Adventures of Tin Tin; 5.55 News; 6.5 Town and Around; 6.30 Going for a Song (antiques quiz that made a star of Arthur Negus)
7.00 Tomorrow's World; 7.35 The Lucy Show; 8.00 King of the River (series); 8.50 News; 9.00 Play: Vote, Vote, Vote for Nigel Barton (by Dennis Potter);
10.20 24 Hours; 10.50 Viewpoint; 11.20 Weather and closedown

BBC2 highlights
8.00 The Dick Emery Show; 8.30 Man Alive

ITV Rediffusion
4.45 Small Time; 5.00 Zoo Time; 5.25 William Tell (Conrad Philips in the title role); 5.55 News; 6.07 Batman; 6.35 Crossroads; 7.00 University Challenge; 7.30 Coronation Street; 8.00 Laredo (Western series); 8.55 News; 9.10 Tom Jones!; 9.40 The Opium Trail; 10.40 Professional Wrestling; 11.25 News; 11.27 World War (with A. J. P. Taylor); 11.57 Dateline; 12.7 Faith and the Word

Chart entries

1st   The Who, 'I'm a Boy' (reached No 2)
8th   New Vaudeville Band, 'Winchester Cathedral' (No 4)
     The Seekers, 'Walk With Me' (No 10)
     Sonny & Cher, 'Little Man' (No 4)
     The Supremes, 'You Can't Hurry Love' (No 3)
15th   Dave Dee, Dozy, Beaky, Mick and Tich, 'Bend It' (No 2)
     Dusty Springfield, 'All I See is You' (No 9)
29th   The Rolling Stones, 'Have You Seen Your Mother, Baby, Standing in the Shadows' (No 5)
     The Troggs, 'I Can't Control Myself' (No 2)

DECLINE OF STEAM. . .

Lines closed

3rd   Scotswood to Prudhoe (West Wylam Junction) via Blaydon
5th   Didcot, Foxhall Junction to North Junction
     Aylesbury to Rugby Central
     Ashendon Junction to Grendon Underwood Junction
     Culworth Junction to Banbury
     Nottingham Victoria to Sheffield (Woodhouse Junction)
     Northam Junction to Southampton Terminus

Loco sheds closed

5th   Keith Junction and Elgin (sub-sheds to Kittybrewster, 61A), Pwllheli (sub-shed to Machynlleth, 6F)

Locomotives withdrawn

The last '1600' Class 0-6-0PT, No 1628 (see page 53), was withdrawn from Croes Newydd on the 10th, the last Fowler 2-6-4T, No 42410, was withdrawn from Huddersfield on the 4th, and the last pair of 'A4' Pacifics', Nos 60019 *Bittern* (saved for preservation - see page 85) and 60024 Kingfisher, were withdrawn from Aberdeen Ferryhill on the 5th. 'WC' 'Pacific' No 34026 *Yes Tor* and 'BB' 'Pacific' No 34066 *Spitfire* (see page 39) were withdrawn from Salisbury on the 18th and 4th respectively. 'MN' 'Pacifics' Nos 35010 *Blue Star* and 35027 *Port Line* were also withdrawn, from Bournemouth, but were rescued for preservation from Barry in 1982, 15 years after their arrival there. No

35029 *Ellerman Lines*, withdrawn from Weymouth on the 11th, spent nearly seven years at Barry before being acquired and 'sectioned' for display in the National Railway Museum, York. The total of 141 locos withdrawn during the month included 27 'Black Fives', 'Jubilee' No 45627 *Sierra Leone*, 17 '8Fs', seven 'V2s' (all but one in Scotland), six 'B1s' (all from Thornton), five Standard '5MT' 4-6-0s, ten Standard '4MT' 2-6-0 of the 76000 series, nine Standard 2-6-4Ts of the 80000 series, nine 'Austerity' 2-8-0s and four '9F' 2-10-0s.

Total steam locos withdrawn in September: 141
Cumulative total for year: 780

Thursday 1 September
During the month I managed to fit in three longer trips, one to North Wales, one to the North West and one to Yorkshire, but first I went over to Nottingham Victoria station before the through workings to Marylebone finished on the 3rd, with the closure of the former GCR London Extension between Rugby and Aylesbury. One of the first workings I saw was '8F' 2-8-0 No 48696 emerging from Mansfield Road Tunnel with a southbound haul of coal.

Later in the day 4-6-0 No 44858 entered Nottingham Victoria with the ECS of the 5.15 pm service to Marylebone, passing the former GCR Victoria North signal box. This is the picture for which I had waited most of the afternoon, and for once the sun did shine.

Thursday 1 September
Above The final picture in this Great Central trio shows No 44858 taking water at the southern end of Victoria station, before leaving for London Marylebone.

Monday 5 September
Left I went up to North Wales, first of all round the Conway Castle area, where I photographed 'Black Five' 4-6-0 No 45042 on a down evening passenger train, probably from Manchester to Bangor.

Tuesday 6 September
Above right I started off photographing on the four-track section between Llandudno Junction and Colwyn Bay, where BR Standard Class '5MT' 4-6-0 No 73157 is seen with a midday Bangor-Manchester train.

Right Later that day I was on the coastal section of the North Wales line around Penmaenmawr, where I saw very clean Class '5' 4-6-0 No 44663, heading west for Bangor with an engineers' special train.

SEPTEMBER

Wednesday 7 September
Left I managed to photograph ex-LNER Class 'B1' 4-6-0 No 61289 as it left Penmaenmawr tunnel with a down afternoon goods.

Saturday 10 September
This page On returning from North Wales, I spent the following Saturday on the SR Waterloo-Basingstoke main line around the Pirbright area. The weather was fine and there was a fair amount of steam activity.

One of the first pictures I took that day (*top*) was of 'Battle of Britain' 'Pacific' No 34067 (formerly *Tangmere*) sweeping round the curves with the 11.30 am Waterloo-Bournemouth.

Later in the day I moved to Deepcut, about a mile or so west of the previous location, and caught No 34032 *Camelford* in charge of the 1.59 pm Bournemouth-Waterloo train as it passed under the aqueduct that carries the Basingstoke Canal over the line. Less than a month later, on 2 October, *Camelford* was withdrawn.

My final picture of that day was of unrebuilt 'West Country' No 34015 *Exmouth* near Deepcut with an up evening passenger train bound for Waterloo.

Monday 12 September

Apart from this afternoon view of No 45447 climbing Grayrigg bank near Lambrigg crossing with a Blackpool-Glasgow holiday extra, the first three full days of my trip to the North West were spent mainly on the Settle & Carlisle route.

Tuesday 13 September

Although the picture on page 4 was taken in sunshine, all the other pictures on the S&C were taken in dull light. This picture of 'Britannia' 'Pacific' No 70009 (formerly *Alfred the Great*) approaching Ais Gill summit with a southbound midday goods is typical of the lighting conditions.

Friday 16 September

When I moved back to the Tebay area on the evening of the 15th the lighting was improving all the time, and the Friday turned out to be a very pleasant early autumn day, with good spells of sunshine. Approaching Grayrigg box on that Friday mid-morning is 'Britannia' 'Pacific' No 70011 (formerly *Hotspur*) with a short southbound parcels train.

Opposite page Later on that afternoon I moved 'round the corner', so to speak, to Dillicar in the Lune Gorge. The first picture shows clean 'Black Five' No 45187 with a down parcels train on the water troughs near the Tebay end where the West Coast Main Line crosses the River Lune.

A short while later I photographed Class '4MT' 2-6-0 No 43033 as it propelled a down ballast train towards Tebay. I was standing on what is now the M6 motorway.

Friday 16 September
This page Moving south to the southern end of Grayrigg bank near Oxenholme, I arrived in time to see 'Britannia' 'Pacific' No 70051 (formerly *Firth of Forth*) with a down evening van train.

Following close on its heels was a down ballast train, hauled by '8F' 2-8-0 No 48731 and banked by Fairburn 2-6-4 tank No 42251.

Tuesday 20 September
Opposite page A few days after returning home from the North West, I made a short trip to Yorkshire. On that hazy Tuesday I photographed Class '5' No 45247 passing Normanton shed (55E) and approaching Normanton station with a coal train.

Wednesday 21 September

Left The following day there was a lot of activity at Wakefield Kirkgate station, including ex-LNER Class 'B1' 4-6-0 No 61237 (formerley named *Geoffrey H. Kitson*) passing through on the outer lines of the station with a westbound coal train. The locomotive lasted only until 6 December, when it was withdrawn from Wakefield shed.

Below left A short while afterwards 2-6-4 tank No 42116 worked out of Kirkgate station with the Bradford portion of an express from King's Cross, the main portion of the train, bound for Leeds, being taken forward by a 'Deltic'.

Right Later that afternoon ex-LMS 'Jubilee' Class 4-6-0 No 45593 *Kholapur* entered Wakefield Kirkgate station with a mixed east-bound goods, a lowly task for such a famous class of express locomotives. By this time, very few 'Jubilees' were still at work and, as can be seen in this book, they could be found on any sort of train. Happily, *Kholapur* is one of a number of 'Jubilees' that have been preserved, and has seen much work on main-line specials, as well as visits to preserved lines.

Monday 26 September

There was still steam at work on the Halesowen-Old Hill branch, and here we see 0-6-0 pannier tank No 4696 (see also page 111) halted by Old Hill Tunnel mouth with a goods for Stourbridge Junction. The train is being banked in the rear by Class '2MT' 2-6-0 No 46442. Twelve days later the 2-6-0 was withdrawn from service at Tyseley shed.

October

THE HEADLINES. . .

The Nobel Prizes are awarded, but there is no Peace Prize winner.

18th The Queen grants a Royal Pardon to Timothy Evans, hanged in 1950 for the murder of his wife and child at 10 Rillington Place, Notting Hill, London. The real murderer, John Christie, was later tried and hanged in 1953.

21st At 9.30 am in Aberfan, Mid Glamorgan, 250 children aged 5 to 11 die when a coal tip slips and engulfs their school.

22nd Britain's David Bryant wins the first World Bowls Championship singles title in Sydney.

23rd George Blake, a leading Russian spy, escapes from Wormwood Scrubs prison where he is serving a 40-year sentence for spying. Thirty years later, in April 1996, British courts decide that Blake can receive the royalties from his book. He is now 73 years old and the £90,000 the UK publisher had been holding will be released to him in Moscow.

ENTERTAINMENT

London theatres

Criterion: 'An Evening with GBS' starring Max Adrian, famous for his impersonation of George Bernard Shaw
Globe: 'There's a Girl in My Soup' starring Donald Sinden and Jon Pertwee

Television: Thursday 6 October

BBC1
Golf all afternoon, then 4.45 Jackanory; 5.00 Blue Peter; 5.25 Tales from Europe; 6.05 Town and Around; 6.30 Man
7.00 United!; 7.40 Top of the Pops; 8.00 Adam Adamant Lives! (Gerald Harper as an Edwardian clubman frozen, then thawed out in modern-day London); 8.50 News; 9.05 The Norman Vaughan Show; 9.30 24 Hours; 9.56 Horse of the Year Show; 10.45 24 Hours; 11.05 A Good Job With Prospects; 11.35 Weather and Roadworks report

BBC2 highlight
Labour Party Conference

ITV Rediffusion
4.45 For Children; 5.00 Junior Criss Cross Quiz; 5.25 The New Forest Rustlers; 5.55 News; 6.07 Reporting '66; 6.35 Crossroads
7.00 Strange Lady in Town (1955 Greer Garson film); 8.55 News; 9.15 This Week; 9.45 Tom Jones!; 10.15 The Frost Programme; 10.55 What the Papers Say; 11.10 News; 11.12 Labour Party Conference; 11.22 T.H.E. Cat, starring Robert Loggia; 11.52 Faith and the Word

Radio highlight

Home
12.00 Call My Bluff

Chart entries

6th Herman's Hermits, 'No Milk Today' (reached No 7)
Paul Jones, 'High Time' (No 4)
13th Bobby Darin, 'If I Were A Carpenter' (No 9)
Four Tops, 'Reach Out I'll Be There' (No 1)
The Hollies, 'Stop Stop Stop' (No 2)
Cliff Richard, 'Time Drags By' (No 10)
27th Lee Dorsey, 'Holy Cow' (No 6)
The Easybeats, 'Friday on my Mind' (No 6)
Manfred Mann, 'Semi-detached Suburban Mr Jones' (No 2)
Jimmy Ruffin, 'What Becomes of the Broken-hearted?' (No 10)

DECLINE OF STEAM. . .

Lines closed

3rd Yatton to Clevedon
Meldon Junction to Wadebridge
Halwill Junction to Bude
Norton Fitzwarren to Barnstaple Junction

Stations closed

3rd Bathampton Halt, Limpley Stoke Halt (Bathampton-Bradford on Avon, GW); Sparkford, Marston Magna, Evershot Halt, Cattistock Halt, Grimstone & Frampton (Castle Cary-Dorchester, GW); Witham (Som) (GW)

Loco sheds closed

3rd Closed to steam: Ayr (67C), Hurlford (67B), Stranraer (67F), Banbury (2D), Kirkby-in-Ashfield (16E), Llandudno Junction (6G), Westhouses (16G)

17th Manchester Agecroft, Liverpool Bank Hall

Locomotives scrapped

On the Isle of Wight No W35 *Freshwater* was withdrawn from Ryde on the 2nd (see page 119). 'WC' 'Pacifics' Nos 34005 *Barnstaple*, 34009 *Lyme Regis*, 34017 *Ilfracombe* and 34032 *Camelford* (see page 141) were also withdrawn on the 2nd, and three 'Britannia' 'Pacifics' were also withdrawn during the month, Nos 70017 *Arrow*, 70036 *Boadicea* and 70044 *Earl Haig*. The acceler-ating pace of loco withdrawals saw the following taken out of service in October: the last two LMS '4F' 0-6-0s, Nos 44377/525, 31 'Black Fives', nine Ivatt '2MT' 2-6-0s (including No 46521, rescued from Barry in March 1971 for use on the Severn Valley Railway), 16 LMS 'Jinty' 0-6-0Ts, 25 '8Fs', seven Standard 4-6-0s of the 73000 series, nine Standard 2-6-0s of the 76000 series, four Standard 2-6-0s of the 78000 series, five 2-6-4Ts of the 80000 series, seven 'Austerity' 2-8-0s and eight '9F' 2-10-0s. They ranged in age from Raven 'Q6' 0-8-0s Nos 63453/59 of 1913 to the '9Fs', some less than ten years old.

Total steam locos withdrawn in October: 163
Cumulative total for year: 943

By the end of September, I was very busy in the music world, working nearly every evening at the Locarno Ballroom, Birmingham, first of all with the Billy Walker, then the Andy Ross Orchestras; during the daytime I was lucky enough to do BBC session work with the Johnny Patrick Orchestra. My time was therefore very limited, but as can be seen I still managed to get out on a few trips, mainly local but occasionally a bit further afield.

Tuesday 4 October
I went up to Croes Newydd shed at Wrexham, but there was not a great deal of activity, although as this picture shows, there were many stored locomotives. Standard Class '4MT' 4-6-0 No 75060 shunts the yard with a rake of coal wagons.

Saturday 8 October
Ken Blocksidge and myself managed to get up to the Copy Pit area, where, amongst other things, we saw 'WD' 2-8-0 No 90382 climbing Copy Pit bank from the northern side with a load of empty coal wagons bound for Todmorden and the West Riding.

Wednesday 12 October
There was still steam activity on the Wolverhampton-Shrewsbury line, and this afternoon I photographed '9F' 2-10-0 No 92152 near Codsall with an up goods train.

Monday 17 October
I visited Chester in a attempt to get a picture of a 'Crab' 2-6-0, as I had heard that there were still one or two at work in the area. From the end of one of Chester's lengthy platforms I managed to get this picture of No 42942 as it ran light through the station on that sunny afternoon. Chester No 3A, one of Chester's many signal boxes, is seen clearly at the back of the locomotive.

The shadows are closing in as Standard Class '4MT' 2-6-0 No 76052 prepares to leave Chester with an afternoon train to Birkenhead. One of Chester's famous gantry signals and signal boxes can be seen through the bridge. It was twilight for No 76052, also, as it was withdrawn from Chester shed on 10 December.

Saturday 29 October

I made two visits to Shrewsbury, on 25 and 29 October, and most of the pictures were used in my 'British Railways Past and Present Special' on the Severn Valley Railway, but not this one, taken on 29 October, of Standard Class '4MT' 4-6-0 No 75029 posing at the north end of the station after bringing in the up 'Cambrian'. The Chester line is straight ahead, and the route to Crewe swings around to the right.

November

THE HEADLINES. . .

9th   Ronald Reagan enjoys a landslide election win for the governorship of California.

24th   Parliament rejects by 1 vote the televising of proceedings.

25th   The first live TV exchange between Australia and Britain lasts 2 hours.

26th   President de Gaulle opens the world's first tidal power station in Brittany.

ENTERTAINMENT

London theatres

Cambridge: 'The Impossible Years' starring David Tomlinson
Garrick: 'The King's Mare', with Glynis Johns and Keith Michell

Television: Friday 18 November

BBC1
4.40 Jackanory; 4.55 Junior Points of View; 5.05 Crackerjack; 5.49 Weather; 5.50 News; 5.58 Town and Around; 6.17 The White Heather Club; 6.40 Look at the Wild West (Australia); 7.05 The Newcomers; 7.30 Harry Worth; 8.00 Vendetta (drama series about the Mafia, or, according to critic Philip Purser, '. . .the Trashia, that vast international conspiracy to flood the television networks of the world with filmed thuggery'); 8.50 News; 9.05 Scrutiny (report on children in hospitals); 9.30 International Amateur Boxing; 10.20 24 Hours; 10.45 Weather; 10.47 Out of Town Theatre

BBC2 highlights
8.40 Wheelbase; 9.05 The Virginian

ITV Rediffusion
4.45 Adventures of Twizzle; 5.00 Disney Wonderland; 5.25 The Jetsons; 5.55 News; 6.08 Ready Steady Go!; 6.35 Crossroads
7.00 Take Your Pick, with Michael Miles; 7.30 Peyton Place; 8.00 Intrigue; 8.55 News; 9.10 Felony Squad (American crime series); 9.35 The Des O'Connor Show; 10.05 The World Tomorrow; 10.35 The Frost Programme; 11.10 News; 11.12 Dateline Westminster; 11.22 Laredo; 12.17 Men of Vision

Chart entries

3rd   The Beach Boys, 'Good Vibrations' (reached No 1)
The Spencer Davis Group, 'Gimme Some Loving' (No 2)
Val Doonican, 'What Would I Be' (No 2)
10th   Tom Jones, 'Green Green Grass of Home' (No 1)
Gene Pitney, 'Just One Smile' (No 8)
17th   The Small Faces, 'My Mind's Eye' (No 4)
24th   The Kinks, 'Dead End Street' (No 5)
The Seekers, 'Morningtown Ride' (No 2)

DECLINE OF STEAM. . .

The withdrawal of the last three '5700' Class 0-6-0PTs from the closed Tyseley shed on the 12th effectively eliminated standard gauge ex-GWR steam from BR.

Lines closed

7th   Glasgow Buchanan Street to Sighthill East Junction
Coatbridge to Rutherglen via Langloan
Oswestry to Gobowen
Gunnislake to Callington

Stations closed

7th   Bentley (GE); Finningham, Mellis, Burston, Tivetshall, Forncett, Flordon, (Haughley-Norwich, GE); Billingham-on-Tees (NER); Glasgow Buchanan Street (CR); Lostock Junction (L&Y); Neilston (Low), Uplawmoor for Caldwell, Lugton, Dunlop, Stewarton, Kilmaurs (GBK - CR&GSW Joint); Radway Green & Barthomley (NS); Stonea (GE); Tutbury, Sudbury, Leigh, Cresswell, Meir (Burton-Stoke, NS)

Loco sheds closed

7th   Tyseley (2A), Glasgow St Rollox (65B)
21st   Nottingham (16D)
26th   Leeds Farnley Junction (55C)

Locomotives withdrawn

As mentioned above, the last '5700' 0-6-0PTs were withdrawn on the 12th following the closure of Tyseley shed (see page 79). 'A2' 'Pacific' No 60530 *Sayajirao* was withdrawn from Dundee on the 19th (see page 104), and two more 'Britannia' 'Pacifics', Nos 70037 *Hereward the Wake* and 70054 *Dornoch Firth*, from Carlisle Kingmoor. Also amongst the 164 locos withdrawn during the month were no fewer than 36 'Black Fives', five Ivatt '2MT' 2-6-0s, 16 LMS 'Jinty' 0-6-0Ts, 18 '8Fs', eight 'B1s', ten 'J38' 0-6-0s (from Thornton and Dunfermline on the 19th/21st), and 30 Standard locomotives of various classes, including eight '9Fs'.

Total steam locos withdrawn in November: 164
Cumulative total for year: 1,107

Friday 4 November
On this murky day 'Black Five' No 45292 throws out a good exhaust as it climbs the steep bank at Amblecote (near Stourbridge) with a Stourbridge Junction-Wolverhampton petrol tank train.

Wednesday 9 November
The weather was much better as I photographed 'Black Five' No 44812 heading north through the fine-looking GWR station at Albrighton with an afternoon Wolverhampton-Shrewsbury goods train.

Wednesday 9 November
Above A few minutes later ex-Crosti-boilered '9F' 2-10-0 No 92020 headed out of Albrighton and up Codsall bank with a Wolverhampton-bound tank train.

Thursday 10 November
Below I went to Albrighton again the following day, but the weather was poor, and the only half-decent picture I obtained was of 4-6-0 No 44762, only a fortnight away from withdrawal from its home shed of Croes Newydd, heading through the station with an afternoon up parcels train.

Saturday 19 November

My final trip of the month was to Copy Pit, where '8F' No 48710 was seen with a heavy northbound goods, banked in the rear by sister 2-8-0 No 48053. This line, situated between Todmorden and Burnley, saw steam activity virtually to the end of steam on BR in August 1968.

December

THE HEADLINES. . .

The 900th anniversary of the founding of Westminster Abbey is celebrated.

12th Francis Chichester completes the longest non-stop solo round-the-world voyage in his 18-ton ketch *Gypsy Moth IV* in 107 days.

ENTERTAINMENT

Exit

15th Walt Disney dies at the age of 65.

London theatres

Criterion: 'Loot' by Joe Orton
Her Majesty's: 'Say Who You Are' with Ian Carmichael
Mermaid: 'The Bedsitting Room', starring Spike Milligan

Television: Saturday 17 December

BBC1
12.45 Sport; 5.15 Juke Box Jury; 5.40 News; 5.50 Dr Who (since 1963, still in his original incarnation of William Hartnell); 6.15 Dixon of Dock Green (1955-76); 7.00 High Adventure: Only Angels Have Wings (1939 Cary Grant film); 8.55 The Val Doonican Show; 9.40 News; 10 Match of the Day (since 1964); 10.45 The Late Show; 11.25 Weather and closedown

BBC2 highlights
9.05 Whicker's World; 10.00 Francis Durbridge presents. . . (thriller series)

ATV
Sport until 4.00 The Rifleman; 4.30 Topo Gigio Comes to Town; 4.55 News; 5.00 Results; 5.15 Professional Wrestling; 6.15 Emergency-Ward 10; 7.10 Counterfeit Plan; 8.40 George and the Dragon (comedy series starring Peggy Mount); 9.10 The Baron (antique dealer Steve Forest is really an undercover agent); 10.05 Drama 67; 11.15 On the Braden Beat; 10.45 Countdown; 12.15 Mountains and Molehills

Chart entries

1st The Supremes, 'You Keep Me Hanging On' (reached No 1)

8th Dave Dee, Dozy, Beaky, Mick and Tich, 'Save Me' (No 4)
Donovan, 'Sunshine Superman' (No 2)
15th Cliff Richard, 'In the Country' (No 6)
The Troggs, 'Any Way That You Want Me' (No 8)
The Who, 'Happy Jack' (No 3)

DECLINE OF STEAM. . .

Lines closed

5th Bury Bolton Street (Radcliffe North Junction) to Clifton Junction
Accrington to Ramsbottom (Stubbins Junction)
Rawtenstall to Bacup
Castleton South Junction to West Junction
19th Leeds City (West Junction) to Farnley Junction

Station closed

5th Pendleton (L&Y)

Loco sheds closed

5th Closed to steam: Machynlleth (6F), Holyhead (6J)
12th Closed to steam: Colwick (16B), Barrow (12C), Carlisle Upperby (12B)

Locomotives withdrawn

The highest monthly total of locos withdrawn during 1966 was in December. The last two Deeley 1907 '0F' 0-4-0Ts, Nos 41528/33, were withdrawn on Christmas Day from store, along with the last five Johnson '1F' 0-6-0Ts of 1878, Nos 41708/34/63/804/835 and the last two LMS '0F' 0-4-0STs of 1932/53, Nos 47001/5, following the termination of the Staveley agreement (see April). The last two Johnson 1899 '3F' 0-6-0Ts, Nos 47201/2, were withdrawn on the 17th. Other 'lasts of class' were 'A2' 'Pacific' No 60532 *Blue Peter* (now preserved - see page 91), and 'V2' No 60836, withdrawn on the 31st from Dundee, the penultimate, No 60831, having been taken out of service from York on the 6th. A further 'Britannia' 'Pacific', No 70018 *Flying Dutchman*, was withdrawn from Carlisle Kingmoor on Christmas Eve.
  Amongst the grand total of 192 locomotives withdrawn in December were eight Ivatt '2MT' 2-6-2Ts, most from Carlisle, 13 Fairburn '4MT' 2-6-4Ts, ten Ivatt '4MT' 2-6-0s (from West Yorkshire), six Ivatt '2MT' 2-6-0s, 19 'Jinty' 0-6-0Ts (of which seven were eventually rescued

from Barry for preservation), 14 '8Fs', and 15 'B1s'. From the Standard fleet, ten '5MT' 4-6-0s were withdrawn (most from Scotland), together with 12 '4MT' 2-6-0s of the 76000 series, three '3MT' 2-6-0s of the 77000 series (all from Stourton on the 7th), five '2MT' 2-6-0s of the 78000 series (all from Shrewsbury), six '4MT' 2-6-4Ts (all from Scotland), four '3MT' 2-6-2Ts (all from Patricroft), and four '9Fs'. One of the latter, No 92134, withdrawn on the 10th from Birkenhead, arrived at Barry

just over ten years since it was built, and spent over 13 years there until being bought for preservation in 1980 as the only surviving single-chimney example.

Total steam locos withdrawn in December: 192
Grand total for year: 1,299.

Tuesday 6 December
Because of pressure of work I was able to make only two trips during the month, the first being to Shrewsbury. At 2.15 pm on that December afternoon Standard Class '4MT' No 75002 enters Shrewsbury station with a northbound goods from the Cambrian direction. The lines to Wolverhampton can be seen on the left-hand side of the picture.

Grimy-looking Standard Class '5MT' No 73097 approaches the north end of the station with a passenger train from Chester. The line to Crewe is on the right-hand side.

Index

Tuesday 6 December
Left To complete these scenes at Shrewsbury, a little earlier Class '5' 4-6-0 No 45132 had made a smoky de̶p̶a̶r̶t̶u̶re with the 3.32 pm to Chester.

Tuesday 13 December
Right My final steam picture of 1966 was taken at Water Orton and shows 4-6-0 No 44845 heading for the Birmingham area with a mixed goods off the Leicester line.

During the year I had travelled many thousands of miles throughout England, Scotland and Wales in my search for steam. Along the way I made new friends and enjoyed the company of my old friends, and almost without exception was made welcome by railwaymen young and old. To them I say a big 'Thank you' for making it such an enjoyable year for me, and one that I will never forget.